W9-AFQ-998

Contents

Introduction

I have spent more than a year writing and researching this pamphlet and a lot has changed in my head in the process. In the beginning I thought these women were "interesting;" I now think they are heroic. Not all of them *accomplished* something in the "male" sense of that term, but every woman who examines herself and her society and tries to grow is heroic to me, because the atmosphere is not conducive to it. We have to overcome incredible odds just to question. All women are, in some way, victims of sexism—whether on the job, in the doctor's office, or at home, and I feel now that every woman's struggle is my struggle. Sexism, like racism, is an institution and there are no individual solutions to what is essentially a political/social problem. Almost every woman in this pamphlet handled her oppression and discovered her "person-ness," but hardly a one has not seen her connection with other women and the necessity to change the social condition. Women are a *group*; we share common bonds of biology and of being put in the same place by society (regardless of how you handle it as an individual). The quality of sexism may have changed slightly over the years, but it is a fact that women are still oppressed and still not able to attain Personhood; as long as one of my sisters is oppressed somewhere in the world, it is my responsibility, in fact, everyone's responsibility, to free her by word and action. Presenting models of strong, brave, thinking, feeling women is a step in that direction.

I would like to acknowledge, with many thanks, the help of Gene Damon, editor of THE LADDER (Box 5025, Washington Sta., Reno, Nevado 89503) who supplied me with hard-to-get information on lesbian women and who offered much support. I would also like to thank my small group: Marie, Lily, Laura, Nina and Susan, for their help and encouragement. I dedicate this, with great love, to my mother.

Kathy Taylor

The Vow

for Anne Hutchinson

sister,
your name is not a household word.
maybe you had a 2 line description
in 8th grade history.
more likely you were left out,
as i am when men converse in my presence.
Anne Hutchinson:
"a woman of haughty & fierce carriage."
my shoulders straighten.
you are dead, but not as dead as you
have been, we will avenge you.
you and all the nameless brave spirits,
my mother, my grandmothers,
great grandmothers (Breen Northcott, butcher's wife,
the others forgotten.) who bore me?
generations of denial & misuse
who bore those years of waste? sisters & mothers
it is too late for all of you. waste
& waste again, life after life,
shot to hell. it will take more
than a husband with a nation behind him
to stop me now.

Generations of Denial

**75 Short Biographies
of Women in History**

Kathryn Taylor

Printed in U.S.A.
Third Printing

Times Change Press
62 W. 14th St., NY NY 10011

SBN 87810-014-8

◀Margaret Fuller
Feminist, Writer & Editor

Emmeline Pankhurst▶
Militant English Suffragist

Frances Wright▶
Feminist, Reformer
& "Freethinker"

◀Belva
Lockwood
Lawyer &
Suffragist

◀Sojourner Truth
Former Slave,
Abolitionist & Feminist

Mary Wollstonecraft▶
Feminist & Writer

Lucretia Mott▲
Feminist & Abolitionist

Suffragists, Feminists and Political Leaders

OLYMPE DE GOURGES
18th Century Feminist

The Declaration of the Rights of Man was adopted by the French Assembly on Aug. 26, 1789, and became the preamble to the French Constitution in 1791. The document asserted the "equality and rights of men" and Olympe de Gourges wrote "The Declaration of the Rights of Woman" in 1790 in answer to its obvious inadequacies. She mimicked the style of the document, the better to point out its weaknesses, and in it demanded equal rights for

7

women before the law and in all other circumstances of public and private life.

ABIGAIL ADAMS
1744-1818/Feminist & Patriot

Abigail Adams advised her husband, the president, of the need to include a women's rights clause in the Declaration of Independence. She said: "Remember all men would be tyrants if they could! If particular care and attention is not paid to the ladies, we are determined to foment a rebellion and will not hold ourselves bound by any laws in which we have no voice or representation."[1]

1. Adelman, Joseph, "Abigail Adams" FAMOUS WOMEN, N.Y.: Ellis, Lonow, 1926, p. 86

Whitney, Janet, ABIGAIL ADAMS, Boston: Little, Brown & Co., 1947

MARY WOLLSTONECRAFT
1759-1797/Feminist & Writer

In 1792, the first "considered statement of feminism" was published: A VINDICATION OF THE RIGHTS OF WOMAN. Its struggling, young author had already written several books (novels, non-fiction, translation, children's books and anthologies) and she wrote "RIGHTS OF WOMAN" as an expansion of the theories of A VINDICATION OF THE RIGHTS OF MEN which she had written in 1790 in answer to Burke's just published REFLECTIONS ON THE REVOLUTION IN FRANCE. She says of the rights of men: "The birthright of men, . . . is such a degree of liberty, civil and religious, as is compatible with the liberty of every other individual with whom he is united in a social compact . . . "[1] and she continued this premise in "RIGHTS OF WOMAN" to say that there cannot be society among *unequals* and a "condition of equality for all mankind (sic) must exist without regard for differences of sex."[2] She hoped to find this "society of equals" in France and this same year, 1792, left England to live in Paris and write a history of the revolution. But the Reign of Terror was hard on freethinkers and she had to live in isolation to escape possible arrest. She met and began to live with with an American expatriate, Gilbert Imlay during this time, and had a child by him in 1794. He abandoned them both and she unsuccessfully attempted suicide, saved by his guilty, but timely, return. He sent her to Scandinavia as "therapy," and there she wrote her LETTERS WRITTEN DURING A SHORT RESIDENCE IN SWEDEN, NORWAY AND DENMARK, published in 1795. When she returned to London, she found Imlay living with an actress and attempted suicide again by jumping off Putney Bridge into the Thames. This time she was rescued by two passing boatmen. Giving up on Imlay, she put her energies into a relationship with William Godwin, one of her "literary circle." They lived together for a short while, and married in 1797. Predictably, it was not a traditional marriage; they lived in separate lodgings but used a common residence in London where they entertained their many mutual friends—Southey, Coleridge, Hazlitt, Shelley, etc. Her daughter (Mary Shelley, who wrote FRANKENSTEIN) was born August 30, 1797, and Wollstonecraft died less than a month later of complications resulting from the birth. She was only 38 years old.

1. Wollstonecraft, Mary, A VINDICATION OF THE RIGHTS OF WOMAN,
2. Wollstonecraft, M., p. 18
Wollstonecraft, Mary, A VINDICATION OF THE RIGHTS OF WOMAN, New York: WW Norton Co., Inc. 1967
Preedy, George, THIS SHINING WOMAN, London: Collins, 1937
[see p.7 for portrait]

LUCRETIA MOTT
1793-1880/Feminist & Abolitionist

The Quakers selected ministers by having the congregation choose those they considered most qualified to be spiritual leaders. In 1821, they elected the 28 year old Lucretia Mott, who eventually gained a reputation as the "greatest woman preacher of her time." An outspoken abolitionist all her life, she frequently spoke publicly where women "were not allowed to." She did so in 1833, in Philadelphia at an abolition convention, and out of this convention came the Philadelphia Female Anti-Slavery Society, with Mott as its secretary. As a recognized leader of the abolition movement, she became in great demand as a speaker both North and South, and often endured mob violence and abuse during her lecture tours. In 1840 she went, as a delegate, to the London Anti-Slavery Convention but was forced, as a woman, to sit silently in the balcony (in the good company of E.C. Stanton) during the proceedings. This event marks the beginning of her committment to the public defense of women's rights. She and Stanton spent the rest of their London stay, together, discussing women's rights, and Mott began speaking out for the cause at every speech she gave on abolition. She was "the first American to publicly advocate equal rights for women."[1] In 1845, at a meeting of Friends (Quakers) in Ohio, she held a special session just for women, advocating equal rights and higher education for women. In 1848, while Mott was visiting a friend (just 10 miles from Seneca Falls), Elizabeth Cady Stanton contacted her and together they planned the first Women's Rights Convention. She gave the keynote address and the movement was launched. In 1866, again in collaboration with Stanton, she created what became known as the most radical wing of the movement, the National Woman Suffrage Association. In 1868, she began to work with peace movements, and became the president of the Philadelphia Peace Society. At the time of her death, she was serving on the executive committee of the society.

1. Stoddard, Hope, FAMOUS AMERICAN WOMEN, p. 325

Cromwell, Otelia, LUCRETIA MOTT, Cambridge: Harvard Univ. Press, 1958
Hare, Lloyd, THE GREATEST AMERICAN WOMEN: LUCRETIA MOTT, N.Y.: American Historical Society, 1937
Stoddard, Hope, "Lucretia Mott" FAMOUS AMERICAN WOMEN, N.Y.: Thomas Y. Crowell, Co., 1970 [see p.7 for portrait]

FRANCES WRIGHT
1795-1852/Feminist, Reformer & "Freethinker"

Although born and raised in Scotland and Britain, Wright had an enthusiasm and involvement in the United States that makes her one of this country's most important feminists and social critics. She first visited the United States in 1818 and in 1821 published a book noted for its unusually "fresh, candid and cogent analysis" of American society and manners. She returned to the U.S. with

Lafayette in 1824, and decided, at that time, to do something about the problems of slavery. Although not strictly an abolitionist, she did feel a non-violent solution to the problem was possible and set out her ideas in the PLAN FOR THE GRADUAL ABOLITION OF SLAVERY in 1825. She had bought a farm in Tennessee and a few slaves to demonstrate her theories (!) but after meeting Robert Owen, the Utopian Socialist, decided to modify her old ideas and make it a truly "communal" farm. She recruited pioneers to work with the now-freed slaves, but scandal ended the experiment. Rumors were spread that free love and racial interbreeding were practiced and social opposition became too violent for Wright to endure. Continuing her connection with Robert Owen, she became co-editor of the "Free Enquirer" in 1829, which promulgated an end to debtors' prison, free state education, and birth control, among many other controversial topics. She was in great demand as a lecturer as a result of her connection with the "Free Enquirer" and always spoke out for women's rights: "Let women stand where they may in the scale of improvement, their position decides that of the race. Are they ignorant?—so is society gross and insipid. Are they wise?—so is the human condition prosperous . . . . Are they enslaved?—so is the whole race degraded."[1]

1. from her "Course of Popular Lecturers" New York: 1830, quoted in VOICES FROM WOMEN'S LIBERATION, p. 34

Tanner, Leslie (ed.) VOICES FROM WOMEN'S LIBERATION, N.Y.: Signet, 1971   [see p.7 for portrait]

SOJOURNER TRUTH
1797-1883/Former Slave, Abolitionist & Feminist

According to a law passed in 1817, all slaves in the north were to be freed by 1827 if they were over 28 at that time. A few months before manumission, Sojourner Truth took things into her own hands and walked down a road near New Paltz, New York and out of slavery forever. In New York City, she worked as a domestic and became involved with some religious fanatics who used her energy, time and savings and eventually implicated her in the bizarre death of one of their leaders. The newspapers were more than ready to respond to a Black woman's involvement in a white man's death with hostility, and they called her a "Black witch." She sued them and won damages of $125. In 1843, she left the city and became a wandering lecturer, carrying the "message from God" she felt herself to have received. She walked up and down the eastern seaboard several times. After staying a short while with some utopian community people in Florence, Massachusetts, she wrote her autobiography and decided to sell it for the cause of abolition and her own life sustenance. It was published in 1850 and proved a useful source of income for the rest of her life (NARRATIVE OF SOJOURNER TRUTH: A NORTHERN SLAVE). It became clear to her, at this time, that she suffered double oppression: as a Black woman. She began speaking out on women's rights and was invited to several conventions by the feminists (despite the opposition of many vocal, powerful racist members). She spent the next five years traveling all over the mid-west and east lecturing on feminism and on non-violence, to whomever would listen. After the Emancipation Proclamation freed southern slaves, she devoted her time to helping freed men and women make it on their own. She taught, and found jobs for the unemployed in the nation's capital. She petitioned Congress to give ex-slaves free land and tools in the west, arguing that this would take them off the charity roles, but no one had the foresight to see the intelligence of what she was proposing. She died having accomplished, at least in some measure, what she had set out to do. Many hundreds were reached with her message of non-violence, abolition and women's rights and were moved to act and speak for positive social change.

Bernard, Jacqueline, JOURNEY TOWARD FREEDOM: THE STORY OF SOJOURNER TRUTH, New York: Dell, 1967 [see p.7 for portrait]

CAROLINE NORTON (Elizabeth Sheridan)
1808-1877/Feminist & Novelist

Her husband charged her with adultery and although he lost his case, was awarded custody of their children and given the right to collect her earnings, which were not inconsiderable—£ 1,400 a year at her peak! Outraged, she wrote a pamphlet, ENGLISH LAWS FOR WOMEN IN THE 19th CENTURY (1854) and a LETTER TO THE QUEEN in 1855. Her protestations and arguments were heard and acted as a catalyst for the few changes that were effected in English marriage laws. She was also concerned with child labor and as early as 1836 wrote a widely publicized poem called A VOICE FROM THE FACTORIES, describing the plight of over-worked children.

Adelman, Joseph, FAMOUS WOMEN, p. 165

MARGARET FULLER
1810-1850/Feminist, Writer & Editor

At the age of thirty, Margaret wrote: "Once I was almost all intellect, now I am almost all feeling. . . . This cannot last long; I shall burn to ashes if all this smoulders here much longer. I must die if I do not burst forth in genius or heroism."[1] Fuller had been a precocious child, knowing Latin at six, reading the "classics" by eight and studying Greek and French in between. Her adolescent years were circumscribed by her family's demands and the need to earn a living, so she taught languages and managed to support herself. Her answer to the problem of realizing her full potential as a creative human being was to start "Conversations" for women (1839) which she called "Feminist Adventures." The result of these conversations, which E.C. Stanton and other feminists attended, was the famous WOMAN IN THE 19th CENTURY published in 1844. This book "prepared the way for the Seneca Falls Convention of 1848 and the woman's rights conventions of the '50's".[2] Her premise: "Women are the best helpers of one another. Let them think; let them act; till they know what they need . . . . I have urged on women independence of man; not that I do not think the sexes mutually needed by one another, but because in woman this fact has led to an excessive devotion, which has cooled love, degraded marriage, and prevented either sex from being what it should be to itself or the other."[3] In addition to her works on feminism, Fuller edited the Transcendentalist magazine, "The Dial," which spoke out for the right of eveyone to be all he, or she, was capable of being. During this period of literary activity she also did reviews for the "Herald Tribune," which were collected into PAPERS ON LITERATURE AND ART. The last four years of her life were spent in Europe, primarily in Italy, where she participated in the Revolution led by Garibaldi. It was at this time she found herself pregnant by an Italian noblemen, ten years her junior, so she married. Their child was born in 1848. She wrote a book about her participation in the Revolution and was returning to America to publish it when her ship was driven onto a sand bar by a gale. She and her husband and child drowned (by some accounts, intentionally) and her manuscript was lost.

1. Anthony, K., p. 6
2. Anthony, K., p. 63
3. Anthony, K., p. 71
Anthony, Katharine, MARGARET FULLER: A PSYCHOLOGICAL BIO-GRAPHY, New York: Harcourt, Brace and Howe, 1920 [see p.7 for portrait]

MARY LIVERMORE
1820-1905/Journalist & Feminist

In addition to being a journalist (and the only woman reporter present at Lincoln's nomination!) Livermore was a Universalist minister, novelist, lecturer and ardent woman suffragist. In 1860, when she was covering Lincoln's nomination in Chicago, she was also editing her husband's paper, acting as correspondent for various other journals, writing books and magazine articles, working in hospitals and delivering occasional lectures on temperance! During the Civil War, she worked with the Sanitary Commission and raised enormous amounts of money for them via speeches, pamphlets and bulletins, in which she described her many trips to the "front." At the war's end, she turned her attention to the burgeoning woman suffrage movement and devoted herself to becoming a one-woman advertisement for the power of the "new" woman. On January 8, 1870, she left her own paper, the "Chicago Agitator" to work with the "Woman's Journal" which she co-edited with Lucy Stone and Stone's husband, Blackwell. This journal represented the American Woman Suffrage Party—the "conservative" reform-oriented opposite of Anthony and Mott's National Party. Livermore, Stone and their followers believed in working via a coalition with men and sought legal rights through gradual change.

Pond, J.B. "Mary Livermore" ECCENTRICITIES OF GENIUS, New York: Dillingham Co., 1900, p. 155
Flexner, Eleanor, CENTURY OF STRUGGLE, New York: Atheneum, 1968, p. 152

BELVA LOCKWOOD
1830-1917/Lawyer & Suffragist

Belva Lockwood was the first woman to plead before the Supreme Court of the U.S., and a candidate for president in 1884 and '88 on the Ticket of the Equal Rights Party (see WOODHULL). While teaching school at $3 a week in Niagara County, New York, she discovered that male teachers were earning twice as much, and she had a baby to support! Outraged, she complained and was told it was "the way of the world." As of that day, she became a life-long committed feminist. She was one of two women graduated in 1873 from the brand new National University Law school in Washington, D.C., and in 1879 she drew up legislation permitting women to practice before the Supreme Court. At this time she was also acting as legal counsel for the suffragists: presenting bills to Congress and often lobbying them through on behalf of the Suffrage party. Her efforts were not limited to suffrage struggles however. Lockwood fought also for the oppressed minorities in America, especially Native Americans and newly freed Black women and men; she proposed admission of Samuel Lowry, Black, to the bar of the Supreme Court, and he was admitted. She won an extremely lucrative case for the Cherokee Indians, involving a 5 million dollar settlement from the government! She developed a national reputation distinct enough that she was often editorialized about, always reviewed (whether a book or lecture) and occasionally ridiculed in cartoon and song. She defied many conventions and died penniless, but revered by her contemporaries as a bulwark against oppression.

Winner, Julia Hull, BELVA LOCKWOOD, Niagara County Historical Society Inc., 1969, No. 9 of the Occasional Contributions [see p.7 for portrait]

EMILY FAITHFUL
1835-1895/English Feminist & Printer

Faithful was extremely interested in the problems of working women and wished to extend their sphere of labor. In 1860, she set up a printing business *for* women, in London, called the "Victoria

Press." She became "publisher in ordinary" to Queen Victoria and in 1863 published a monthly magazine called "The Victoria Magazine" in which, for 18 years, she advocated the rights of women to equal pay for equal work.

Adelman, Joseph, FAMOUS WOMEN

TSIN KING
20th Century/ Chinese Feminist

Founder of a semi-monthly magazine for women and a modern school for girls in China, she was executed in 1907 during political persecution of progressive intellectuals.

Schirmacher, Kaethe, THE MODERN WOMEN'S RIGHTS MOVEMENT,New York: MacMillan Co., 1912

EMMELINE PANKHURST
1857-1928/Militant English Suffragist

In 1903, she founded the Women's Social and Political Union as an organizing tool to gain woman suffrage in Britain. She and her followers struggled patiently for years, "asking" men for the vote, but in 1911, she innaugurated a new era of violence and militancy. She organized a window-breaking campaign and in 1912 was arrested for inciting to violence. From 1913-1914, she and her followers "fired" the country—burning homes, railroad stations, churches, and government buildings; they bombed civil buildings and fought the police in hand-to-hand combat in the streets! Thousands of women were put in jail and many went on hunger strikes to protest their treatment, often being brutally force fed by the authorities. She called a brief retreat in 1914 to help in the war effort, and in 1918, the Representation of the People Act granted suffrage to women over 30. She died the year women were given full enfranchisement, 1928. Her daughters carried on her struggle for equality: Christabel became a lawyer and fought for admittance to the bar, and Sylvia became a pacifist, active in international pacifist movements.

Adelman, Joseph, FAMOUS WOMEN, p. 289

de Morny, Peter, "Emmeline Pankhurst" THE BEST YEARS OF THEIR LIVES, London: Centaur Press, Ltd., 1955, P. 163 [see p.7 for portrait]

SAROJINI NAIDU
1879-1949/Indian Poet & Political Leader

Educated at Madras University and London, she wrote volumes of widely translated poetry: THE GOLDEN THRESHOLD (1905), THE BIRD OF TIME (1912) and THE BROKEN WIND (1915). Naidu began her political career in 1905 when she addressed the All-Indian Social Conference in Calcutta. In 1919 she became a follower of Ghandi and was jailed several times for civil disobedience. In 1925, she became the first woman president of the Indian National Congress. During WW II, she again supported Ghandi in his resistance to the British and was jailed for it from 1942-43. After India attained dominion status in 1947, she served as governor of the United Provinces until her death. In all of her activities, Naidu strove to improve the status of women, offering her own political activism as an example to both men and women, of what women could achieve.

[see cover for portrait]

LEILA MAHMEDBEKOVA
20th Century/First Airwoman in Soviet Turkey

As late as 1928, Leila Mahmedbekova was still wearing the traditional veil, demanded by Turkish men to protect their "property" from jealous eyes. Near the end of the decade she entered aviator's school and eventually became an expert Airwoman, teaching men and women to fly. Other Turkish women quickly followed her example and it became a popular profession for women. SULEIKA MAHMEDOVA was one such woman, who was in addition, the first woman parachutist in Soviet Turkey and a mining engineer!

Green, Margaret, WOMEN IN THE SOVIET EAST, N.Y.: Dutton & Co., Inc., 1938, p. 290-1.

See Also: Mary M. Bethune, Anne Hutchinson, Jane G. Swisshelm, Mary Lease, Margaret Sanger, Mary Somerville, Anna Dickinson, Maria Mitchell, George Sand, L.M. Alcott, Victoria Woodhull, Tajikhan Shadiyeva.

◀ Joan of Arc
Visionary,
Military Leader
& Witch

◀ Godiva
Heroine

Anna Dickinson
Orator ▼

◀ Edith Cavell
Nurse & Martyr

Military Leaders, Queens, Martyrs, Heroines and Lesbians

BOADICEA
d. 62 AD/Queen & Military Leader

She was Queen of Norfolk in eastern Britain. After her husband's death, his family was put under the protection of the Roman emperor who immediately tried to confiscate all their land and money. Boadicea resisted this robbery and was caught, stripped and beaten. Her daughters were raped. Seeking revenge, she led the Britons in an attack on Colchester, London and St. Albans and 70,000 Romans were slaughtered. In retaliation, C. Suetonius Paulina, a Roman general, and 10,000 men, attacked her forces. She and her daughters led the defense from chariots, but were over-run and defeated. She died a short time later—possibly from poison.

King, William, "Boadicea" WOMAN, Springfield, Mass.: The King-Richardson Co., 1902, p. 120.

JUDITH
d. 977/ Queen of the Falashas or Black Jews

As a warrior queen, Judith attacked Axum, the sacred capital of Ethiopia and captured it in 937 AD. By this report, she killed, sparing none, members of the family of Solomon and the Queen of Sheba. She conquered all but a small portion of Ethiopia and ruled it until her death in 977.

Rogers, J. A., WORLD'S GREAT MEN OF COLOR, Vol. II, New York,1947

GODIVA
c. 1050 /Heroine

Godiva's husband was the powerful Earl of Mercia (Lord of Coventry). The people under his rule pleaded with her to intercede on their behalf with the Earl, to get the excessively heavy taxes lowered. He jokingly offered to lower them if she would ride naked through the town. She agreed and did so. According to some accounts, he fulfilled his promise, in "admiration."

Adelman, Joseph, "Lady Godiva" FAMOUS WOMEN, New York: Ellis Lonow Co., 1926, p. 32. [see p. 18 for portrait]

PHILIPPA OF HAINAULT
1312-1369/Military Leader & Educator

In 1346, she led 12,000 men in battle against the invading Scots and defeated them, capturing their king, David Bruce. In addition, she founded Queens College, Oxford and established a manufacturing colony of Flemish workmen at Norwich in 1335. This colony manufactured cloth and made it available to merchants—the first step toward mass production of clothing.

King, William, "Philippa of Hainault" WOMAN, Springfield, Mass.: The King-Richardson Co., 1902, p. 202.

JOAN OF ARC
1412-1431/Visionary, Military Leader & Witch

Her first visions came when she was 12 and she believed them to be from Saints Michael, Margaret and Catherine. They told her to drive the English out of France and put the Dauphin (later Charles

VII) on the throne. England at that time occupied all of northern France after victories at Agincourt, Crécy and Poitiers. She waited, watched and thought for four years, and finally, at 16, sought the Dauphin. It took her eight months more to convince the Dauphin's commandant of her seriousness. To avoid sudden attack on the road, she disguised her sex by cutting her hair short and dressing as a man. Presumably she found it more convenient and suited to her personality because she never voluntarily returned to woman's dress. In 1429, she set out at the head of 10,000 troops to raise the siege of Orleans. She added to her already mythic stature by wearing armor, riding astride a white charger and leading her troops in hand-to-hand combat. Although wounded by an arrow, she raised the siege and was found, after the battle, praying on the field for the English and French dead. Joan defeated the English in battle after battle, despite "ignorance" of conventional war tactics—or perhaps because of it. The arrogant generals were taken by surprise by her unorthodox and unpredictable lines of attack. She was eventually captured by a dissident French faction (Burgundians) and sold to the English in 1431. The ungrateful Dauphin wouldn't ransom her and let her rot in the English prison for months. The English tried her for four months, finally accusing her of heresy and witchcraft. They burned her alive at Rouen, May 30, 1431. Charles VII had her sentence annulled in 1456, in belated recognition and gratitude. She was canonized by an equally guilty church in 1920. Much has been written about Joan, but of particular note: A biography by Victoria Sackville-West in 1936 and George B. Shaw's play, SAINT JOAN.

Foss, Kenelm, "Joan of Arc" UNWEDDED BLISS, Kingswood: The World's Work, Ltd., 1949, p. 150. [see p. 18 for portrait]

LOUISE LABÉ
1525-1566/Poet & Lesbian

Her sonnets, considered "some of the best love poems in French literature," were printed in 1555 and gained a wide readership. She fought on horseback in the ranks of the Dauphin at the siege of Perpignan and dressed in men's clothes, gaining for herself the title: "La Capitaine Louise." She led somewhat of a double life—one as the traditional "gracious and dignified" housewife and the other as a tempestuous, poetic, openly lesbian, radical woman. She announced, ". . . in the first of her autobiographical elegies . . . that Phoebus had filled her with 'ardor' and had given her the lyre of the amorous Lesbian."[1]

1.Koven, Anna, WOMEN IN CYCLES OF CULTURE, p. 170.
Koven, Anna, "Louise Labé" WOMEN IN CYCLES OF CULTURE, New York: GP Putnam's Sons, 1941, p. 164ff.
Adelman, Joseph, "Louise Labé" FAMOUS WOMEN, New York: Ellis Lonow Co., 1926, p. 47.

NZINGHA (ANN ZINGHA)
1582-1663/ Amazon Queen of Matamba, West Africa

Nzingha grew up during the time the Portuguese were attempting to colonize Angola, West Africa and succeeding beyond their wildest dreams. Nzingha declared them her enemy and organized and trained an army of women warriors, Amazons, whom she led in battle against the colonial oppressors. They matched spears and bows and arrows to the Portuguese rifles and pistols. In the end they lost, but it was only the first of many battles. In l622 she was sent, by her brother, a King, to arrange a peace treaty with the Portuguese viceroy at Loanda. She proved a shrewd, unbribable diplomat and engineered an agreement that did *not* create an alliance with them and which refused to pay tribute to the King of Portugal — all to the satisfaction of the viceroy. About this time she adopted Christianity and some European customs (which she maintained for several years). When her brother died, she took the throne (killing her nephew for it, by some accounts). When she became the ruling party, the Portuguese decided not to honor the treaty she had helped negotiate. They feared her intractability, candidness and honesty and plotted to remove her from the throne. They sent an army against her and she in turn sent her Amazons, allied herself with the Dutch and other chiefs in the area, and fought a war of many years duration. The Portuguese again won, but agreed to leave her on the throne if she would pay tribute to the King. She refused and fled into the jungle where she and her army fought the invaders for the next eighteen years. During this period of total disillusionment with the Europeans, she dropped Christianity and killed any of her followers who did not do the same. At 70, with most of the wars over, she again adopted the church and abolished the sacrifice of captives and criminals, and prohibited polygamy. Even at this age however, she refused to pay tribute to the Portuguese king. When she died, at 81, her body was put on display in her royal robes and in her hands she had her bow and arrows placed; but when she was buried she was dressed, at her own dying request, in the habit of a nun with a rosary and crucifix in her hands. After her death, Angola fell totally to the Portuguese.

Rogers, J. A. , WORLD'S GREAT MEN OF COLOR, Vol. I New York, 1947

A NOTE ON THE AMAZONS OF WEST AFRICA (19th Century)

A great deal of emotional brouhaha surrounds the question of Amazons — real or imaginary, fact or myth — no one seems sure (at least in the media) but scholars have dug up some *facts* : In Dahomey, in the 19th Century, the King's army was composed of 2200 female warriors (out of an army of 3000!) — Amazons, by European description. They had their own separate organization within the larger army, with their own female officers, and were not responsible to the male army, only to the King. The main two divisions were: the standing army and the reserve. The latter served as palace and city guards, especially during war-time. The standing army was divided into three groups: The Left Wing, Right Wing (each commanded by female officers equal in rank to the equivalent males) and the Fanti. The Fanti served as the royal bodyguards, the *élite corps*, consisting of the "famed elephant huntresses, the boldest and toughest of the Amazons." All the Amazons wore a variation of the men's dress, "sleeveless tunics with blue and white stripes, baggy breeches held in at the waist by cartridge belts." Those who were members of the king's bodyguard wore headbands of white ribbon embroidered with a blue crocodile! The individual companies within the above structure were distinguished by the arms they carried: bayonets, muskets, bows and arrows (the latter carried by the youngest recruits). The King recruited the Amazons from among free Dahomeans and captives. He forbade them to marry until middle-age (and then only with his consent), and required them to be celibate. They were equal with the men it seems, except in matters of sex. . .

WEST AFRICAN KINGDOMS IN THE 19th CENTURY, Ed. with introduction by Daryll Forde and P. M. Kaberry.   This is from "The Kingdom of Dahomey" by J. Lombard, p. 70-92. p. 70-92.   (Oxford Press, England, 1967)

CHRISTINA OF SWEDEN
1626-1689/Lesbian & Queen

As a child, Christina was taught to ride, hunt, fence, and shoot, and by 13, she was a scholar who knew Greek, mathematics, astronomy, history and philosophy. She became an accomplished linguist, learning German, Italian, Spanish and French on her own. Her quick and agile mind attracted the intellectuals of the day to her court and at least one, Descartes, remained with her in the frozen north. She ascended the throne in 1644, at the age of 18 and had herself crowned "King." During her reign she freely gave away money and title lands and by the end of her ten years, half of the crownlands were in other hands than the monarch's. In 1654, bored, she abdicated, abandoning Sweden as an "abode of ignorance." It was not totally unwelcome since the Queen had begun her conversion to Catholicism by this time and the staunchly Protestant Swedish public found this heretical. After abdicating, she made a pilgrimage to Rome, and arrived in a dramatic flurry, dressed in men's clothes—which she found more suitable, convenient and comfortable. Her appearance gave added fuel to the fiery storm that raged over the Queen's affection for her court favorite, Ebba (Belle) Sparre. Christina generally introduced Belle as her "bedfellow" and "one whose mind was as beautiful as her body," and both Protestants and Catholics found this a little too forthright for their taste. During her stay in Rome she maintained an enormous correspondence with intellectuals of the time, founded academies, compiled a startling library and collected antiques and paintings. In her later years, she attempted to return to the field of her former glory and schemed to become queen of Poland, Naples and in 1660, tried to regain the throne of Sweden. She tried again, in 1667, to return to the throne, but the damage had been done—her religion was wrong and her candid nature was not appreciated. She died of diabetes in Rome, 1689. M. L. Goldsmith did a psychological study of Christina in 1933, CHRISTINA OF SWEDEN.

Brooks, E. S. "Christina of Sweden" HISTORICAL GIRLS, New York:GP Putnam's Sons, 1897, p. 192.

Masson, Georgina, QUEEN CHRISTINA, NY: Farrar, Straus & Giroux, 1968. [see cover for portrait]

ANNA ELLA CARROLL
1815-1893
Military Genius & "The Unofficial Member of Lincoln's Cabinet"

Ulysses S. Grant has gained much glory and prestige as the alleged mastermind behind the strategy that won the Civil War, the "Tennessee Plan;" but this was a fiction set up and maintained by the War Department, afraid the public would lose confidence in the government if it became known a "mere woman" had evolved the strategy while men bickered and dawdled in political backbiting. This woman was Anna Carroll of Maryland. By the age of 18, she was able to earn her way as a legal consultant and political "confidante" to some of the most powerful political figures of her state. She wrote books, pamphlets and articles on the state of American politics, acted as press agent for the "Know Nothing Movement" and did espionage for the Union. In this latter capacity she collected several documents primarily letters, proving conclusively that Jefferson Davis and others, conspired, as early as 1849 to create a Southern United States. Her activities attracted the attention of Lincoln, who commissioned her to write a brief on his war powers, sent her on a mission to the west to investigate the loyalty of various generals and asked her to evaluate the union plan of attack (which was down the Mississippi River). During this trip, she evolved the Tennessee Plan which foreign and domestic presses hailed as the one which won the war. She was never given recognition for her monumental achievement except for a pension which she would not accept because it did not recognize her part in the winning of the war in anything but a peripheral way.

Noble, Hollister, WOMAN WITH A SWORD, Chicago: The People's Book Club, 1948.

Blackwell, Sarah, A MILITARY GENIUS: THE LIFE OF ANNA ELLA CARROLL OF MARYLAND (1891).

Greenbie, Marjorie B. MY DEAR LADY (1940)

And for a contemporary newspaper account see the reprinted "Editorial from the 'National Citizen,' Syracuse, N.Y., Sept. 1881" in:
Tanner, Leslie, compiled and edited by, VOICES FROM WOMEN'S LIBERATION, N.Y.: New American Library, 1971, p. 85.
[see cover for portrait]

ANNA DICKINSON
1843-1932/Orator

She was called the Union's "Joan of Arc" in recognition of her startling ability to create a "cyclone of patriotic enthusiasm" in the wake of her speeches. Everywhere she spoke, enlistments followed. At twenty-one, she addressed Congress, with Lincoln in attendance and suffragist friends in the balcony. The Congressmen were charged an admittance fee to their own chamber and the proceeds were given, at her request, to the National Freedman's Relief Bureau. It was a rabble-rousing speech and gained her such publicity that she was in enormous demand as a speaker for years afterward. She became known as the "Queen of the Lyceum"—a lecture circuit which booked nationally prominent speakers to lecture on public issues. She joined the esteemed company of Susan B. Anthony, Henry Ward Beecher, Charles Sumner, Ralph W. Emerson and many others. By 1872, she was earning $23,000 a year! This phenomenal income enabled her to live as she pleased: "She dressed as she desired; she traveled where and how she willed; she delivered lectures on subjects many people felt should not even be mentioned in the presence of unmarried young ladies."[1] Susan Anthony considered her a friend and Anna never missed an opportunity to speak out for the suffragist's cause. Eventually the lyceum became a less popular forum for news reportage and analysis than newspapers, and her downhill slip began. She spend a brief period on the stage but was not a success, and as she attempted to come to grips with her increasing obscurity, she became more and more eccentric, causing her sister to attempt to have her committed to an insane asylum. She fought it (in a heavily publicized court case) and won, but never fully recovered from the battle. She died in penury at 90.

1. *Chester, Giraud, EMBATTLED MAIDEN, p. 86.*
Chester, Giraud, EMBATTLED MADIEN, NY: GP Putnam's Sons, 1951
Pond, J.B., "Anna Dickinson" ECCENTRICITIES OF GENIUS, N.Y.: Dillingham Co., 1900, p. 152. [see p. 18 for portrait]

EDITH CAVELL
1865-1915/Nurse & Martyr

During the first world war, the Germans invaded Belgium and over-ran Cavell's school for nurses at the Berkendael Medical Institute. Her school became a Red Cross hospital and she treated *all* wounded there, whether Belgian, English, French or German. She permitted her hospital to be used, however, as a stop on the underground railroad carrying French and British soldiers safely to Holland. Since she openly raised money for their aid, her partisanship was clear, and on August 5, 1915, she was arrested and put in prison. On October 12, 1915, she was shot by a German firing squad for her political activities. In England she was regarded as a martyr and a statue was erected near Trafalgar Square in her memory. Helen Judson wrote her biography in 1941.
[see p. 18 for portrait]

ANNA JAMAL
d. 1927/Martyr to Soviet Turkish Women's Emancipation

Most of Anna Jamal's life was spent doing the traditional tasks of oppressed women in Soviet Turkey: grinding meal, spinning, weaving, laboring in the fields, childbearing and maintaining total and complete subservience to all men—especially husband, father and brothers. She wore a veil as was proscribed and dressed in the heavy, body concealing clothes demanded by the patriarchal society that jealously regarded her as property. In the early 1920's she rebelled: she joined the Communist Party and began traveling and organizing her sisters. She gave talks about resisting the dehumanizing labor and subservient role playing Turkish women had accepted for centuries. She was called "one possessed by the devil," a witch, and village men forbade their wives to speak or listen to her. One night, in 1927, several Turkmen stole into her room, mutilated her children and murdered her. They were eventually caught, tried and shot for their act, and aroused women all over Turkey vowed to carry on her work.

Green, Margaret, WOMEN IN THE SOVIET EAST, NY: Dutton & Co., Inc., 1938, pp. 198-200

See also: Charlotte Corday, Bridget Bishop/Abigail Hobbs, Hester Stanhope, Harriet Hosmer, Pauline Cushman, Rosa Bonheur, George Sand.

Witches

TITUBA
c. 1692

In 1692, a warrant was sworn out for the arrest of Tituba as a witch, on the word of three little girls, whose household she worked in as a slave. Her indictment was a surprise to no one. Of all those accused in the community, she was the most "suspect;" she practiced herbal medicine and knew spells and magic. She seemed to be the first to hit on almost the only defense possible for an accused witch at the time—confession. For three days, she gave the eager people of Salem Village exactly what they wanted to hear, using her imagination freely. She told of witch's sabbaths, orgies, of serving cats and rats, and of a "tall man" who brought out a book with nine names. This threw Salem into a panic since only three witches had been brought to trial! Eventually she was released, for lack of evidence, and became the property of the person willing to pay her prison fees!

Petry, Ann, TITUBA, New York: Thomas Y. Crowell Co., 1964

BRIDGET BISHOP & ABIGAIL HOBBS

They were indicted as witches in Salem Village because they were odd: Bridget wore a red bodice and kept a tavern where she was up late hours and Abigail took long rambles in the woods at night. Abigail plunged into confessing—gaining much support from those she entertained with her stories, but eventually the court couldn't believe her flamboyant tales of murder and torture and became convinced she was innocent. Bridget denied even having knowledge of what a witch was; her insouciant attitude was not favorably received. They were both sent to prison where they were subjected to a humiliating physical search for witch-marks. Bridget was hanged and Abigail got off, and was given £ 10 for her troubles in 1702 by a penitent state of Massachusetts.

Starkey, Marion, THE DEVIL IN MASSACHUSETTS, N.Y.: Alfred Knopf, 1949.

See Also: Joan of Arc

◄ Elizabeth
Gurley Flynn
Union Organizer
"The Rebel Girl"

Charlotte Corday
French Patriot & Martyr

Angelica Balabanoff
Russian Revolutionary

Margaret Sanger
Birth Control
Pioneer

Dolores Ibarruri
Spanish Revolutionary
"La Pasionaria"

Constance Markievicz
Irish Revolutionist

Rosa Luxemburg
Revolutionary

Reformers and Revolutionaries

ANNE HUTCHINSON
1590-1643/Revolutionary

The Puritans were almost as intolerant as those they fled in England, and in the Massachusetts Bay Colony, church and state were even more closely bound than in the "mother" country. Anne Hutchinson, who arrived in the colony in 1634, was an "independent" religious thinker, and her house quickly became a social center where people of intellect and inquiring spirit knew they were welcome. She began having Sunday meetings for women, to discuss and criticize the day's sermon. Forty to one hundred women regularly came, often travelling great distances to hear her commentary and voice their own thoughts. (Women were excluded from the usual after-church group discussions.) Anne began preaching the "covenant by grace" by which she meant the spirit of God was in everyone and inward revelations of the spirit and conscious judgment of the mind were more important than blind submission to church doctrine and authority. With her as a model, her followers began arguing with clergymen during sermons, and actually went so far as to walk out if they were not allowed free speech. She was such a threat to the church that it was deemed necessary to call the first synod in America, in 1637, and all the clergy and magistrates of Massachusetts gathered in Cambridge to meet for three weeks to discuss her "opinions." They immediately condemned her women's meetings as "disorderly and without rule," and in October brought her to trial. It was civil, judicial and ecclesiastical and lasted two days, and she was made to stand through most of it although pregnant and ill. It was a judicial farce and when they were unable to legally prove anything, they were reduced to a juvenile rant: "We are your judges, and not you ours, and we must compel you to it."[1] ("it" being *their* will). An ecclesiastical court excommunicated her, and in March, 1638 she was banished. She and seventy friends went to Roger Williams' Rhode Island and later to the shores of Long Island Sound where she and sixteen members of the colony were killed in a Indian raid in 1643.

1. *quoted in WOMEN IN AMERICAN HISTORY, "Anne Hutchinson" by Grace Humphrey*

Humphrey, Grace, "Anne Hutchinson" WOMEN IN AMERICAN HISTORY, Indianapolis: Bobbs-Merril Co., 1919, p. 18ff [see p.5 for portrait]

MARGARET BRENT
1600-1671?

In 1638, she and her sister arrived in Maryland and as friends of the influential Calvert family, were given "manors" (of 1000 or more acres) which they owned in their own names (in a time when few women could own anything!) In 1647, her brother-in-law, Gov. Leonard Calvert, appointed her the sole executor of his estate. After his death, she appealed to the Maryland Assembly for the right to vote, as a land owner and executor of the governor's estate. They denied her the right even though she was one of Maryland's largest landowners; she had enlarged her holdings over the years, by skillfully managing the estates of absentee planters.

Dexter, Elisabeth, COLONIAL WOMEN OF AFFAIRS, Boston: Houghton-Mifflin, 1931

SUSANNA WESLEY
1669-1742/The Mother of Methodism

John Wesley is credited with founding Methodism, but he learned it from his mother. She had nineteen children in twenty years and taught all of them in the kitchen of their home. She wrote her own texts and taught by rigid rules—"methods." She knew Greek, Latin, French, logic and metaphysics and was passionately interested in debating religious theories. Susanna held services in her kitchen for her children and local servants and eventually huge audiences gathered to hear her read a sermon, say prayers and discuss theology. These gatherings were in violation of the law, but she considered it an immoral law and paid no attention to it. When Methodist societies were formed, John Wesley often sought her advice and guidance on how to run them, and when she died, he acknowledged his debt to her in a sermon.

Adelman, Joseph, "Susanna Wesley" FAMOUS WOMEN, New York: Ellis Lonow Co., 1926, p. 69

Lotz, Philip, "Susanna Wesley" WOMEN LEADERS, New York: Association Press, 1940, p. 118 [see cover for portrait]

MERCY WARREN
1728-1814/American Patriot

Abigail Adams and Mercy Warren were the "early predecessors of S.B. Anthony and E.C. Stanton in voicing and urging the rights of women as individuals and citizens," but their voices were temporarily lost in the wave of revolutionary fervor sweeping the country at that time. Mercy was a committed revolutionist all her life. It was her brother, James Otis, who first articulated the idea that taxation without representation was tyranny, and from the beginning, she was in the thick of the theorizing that led eventually to the War. Her home was a gathering place for revolutionaries and John Adams—later to become president—spent many hours by her fire talking over his ideas with her and with her husband, James Warren. Unable to openly, publicly participate, Mercy put her ideas to work in political satires (poems and plays) and had them printed (anonymously at first) and circulated among Boston patriots. They quickly became underground "classics" passed from hand to hand

and discussed avidly by her audience. Mercy and Adams began to quarrel in 1788 over his repressive response to Shay's Rebellion. Shay, a Revolutionary War veteran, felt that things were not moving fast enough under the government he'd fought to establish, and he and his followers were brutally suppressed by what amounted to private armies (since there were no government provisions yet to deal with civil rebellion). The rift widened that same year, over the issue of ratification of the Constitution. It had been drawn up in "secret by a few of the Boston elite" and Mercy and other Anti-Federalists (as they were called) strongly objected to this undemocratic procedure. In addition, the Constitution seemed to them a document designed to protect property rather than people's rights, and they insisted on a Bill of Rights. Rather than split the union, a compromise was reached and the Bill of Rights was added as ten amendments. Mercy was eventually reconciled with Adams, a rabid Federalist, but it took many, many years. Her crowning achievement was her HISTORY OF THE RISE, PROGRESS AND TERMINATION OF THE AMERICAN REVOLUTION, published in 1805. The culmination of over twenty years of work, it was the first written by an American historian and was widely read, particularly for its "vivid character sketches of leading figures." Her biography has been written by Alice Brown (1896) among others.

Anthony, Katharine, FIRST LADY OF THE REVOLUTION, N.Y.: Double-day & Co., Inc., 1958 [see cover for portrait]

CHARLOTTE CORDAY
1768-1793/ French Patriot & Martyr

After the Revolution, Corday became increasingly upset as Marat and others ordered the executions of thousands during the Reign of Terror. She felt that there had been enough bloodshed and went to Marat with a list of suspected Girondists to see what he would do. When he immediately ordered their execution, she decided to act, and plunged a knife into him, killing him instantly. She was arrested, tried, convicted and guillotined in one day. Adam Lux wrote a pamphlet suggesting a statue to her memory and was guillotined, and Andre Chenier, a poet, wrote a poem praising her heroism and was also executed.

Adelman, Joseph, "Charlotte Corday" FAMOUS WOMEN, New York: Ellis Lonow, Co., 1926, p. 93
Shearing, Joseph, THE ANGEL OF THE ASSASSINATION (1935)
[see p. 28 for portrait]

ELIZABETH FRY
1780-1845/Quaker Prison Reformer

She became a minister in 1810, and in the course of her work in this capacity, she visited Newgate's Women's Prison and was appalled by conditions under which the incarcerated women and children lived. She was responsible for having them provided with the basic necessities such as soap and adequate clothing, and organized "occupational therapy" for them making dresses and quilts. At that time, laws demanded the death penalty for over two hundred crimes ranging from murder to stealing a loaf of bread. She publicized the injustice of killing someone because they stole to fill a hungry belly or clothe a cold body, and advanced the new concept that prison terms were not for revenge, but to "lessen crime and reform the criminal."

Adelman, Joseph, "Elizabeth Fry" FAMOUS WOMEN, New York: Ellis Lonow Co., 1926, p. 136
de Morny, Peter, THE BEST YEARS OF THEIR LIVES, London: Centaur Press, Ltd., 1955, p. 117

JANE GREY SWISSHELM
1815-1884/Editor, Abolitionist & Feminist

In 1848, she established the "Pittsburgh Saturday Visitor," an anti-slavery newspaper and edited it (sometimes from afar) until 1857. In 1850 she was Washington correspondent for Horace Greeley's "Tribune" and got herself into the Senate Press gallery "establishing a woman's right to sit as a reporter"[1] in Congress. In 1857, she started editing another abolitionist paper in Minnesota and her fervent and articulate editorials enraged the community of St. Cloud. A vigilante group invaded her office, destroyed her press and threw her type into the river. She spoke out at anti-slavery rallies and on "woman and politics" even though she suffered much abuse at the hands of bigots. During the Civil War, she was a tireless nurse and single-handedly saved 182 badly wounded men when no doctor was avilable. She also became the first woman to serve in the War Department, where she said she was on "the advance post on the picket line of civilization."[2] She wrote her autobiography, HALF A CENTURY, in 1880.

1. Sillen, Samuel, *WOMEN AGAINST SLAVERY, p. 93*
2. Sillen, *WOMEN AGAINST SLAVERY, p. 99*
Adelman, Joseph, "Jane Swisshelm" FAMOUS WOMEN, p. 167
Sillen, Samuel, "Jane Swisshelm" WOMEN AGAINST SLAVERY, New York: Masses & Mainstream, 1955, p. 93-99

ANITA GARIBALDI
1821-1894/ Brazilian Native, Heroine of Italian Independence

This Brazilian-born heroine of the Italian struggle for independence was considered "an expert rider" and was captain of her husband Garibaldi's legion and "rode into battle beside him." In 1932 a monument was dedicated to her in Rome, by the King of Italy and Mussolini.

Rogers, J. A., WORLD'S GREAT MEN OF COLOR, Vol. II, New York, 1947

LOUISE MICHEL
1830-1905/French Anarchist

She received a liberal education thanks to a wealthy grandfather and taught school in Montmartre in 1866—where she evolved her revolutionary politics. At the end of the Franco-Prussian war in 1871, Parisians protested the readiness of Adolphe Thiers, the head of the national government, to make peace with Prussia, and they set up a Communal government in 1871. Michel, one of their prominent and most radical leaders, offered to personally assassinate Thiers, and suggested the destruction of Paris by way of vengeance for his surrender to the Prussians. She was with the Communards when they made their last stand against the Versaille troops (Thier's supporters) at a cemetary in Montmartre. Reprisals were bloody and 17,000 men, women and children (estimated) were executed. She was arrested and brought before a court where she bravely defended the Paris Commune and defied the judge. Michel was banished and sent as a convict to New Caledonia. She was returned after the amnesty of 1880, but soon imprisoned again for practising her radical politics.

Thomas, Edith, THE WOMEN INCENDIARIES (Women in the Paris Commune)   [see cover for portrait]

CATHERINE BRESHKOVSKAYA
1844-1934/"Grandmother of the Russian Revolution"

Although born a noblewoman, Breshkovskaya became prominent, by 18, as a vocal agitator for serf's rights, against the Tsar. After the liberation of the peasants in 1861, she turned her effort to crusading for education for the peasants. Breshkovskaya set up village schools, libraries, and hospitals, and this brought her to the attention of the Tsar's authorities who arrested her in 1874 and sentenced her to four years in Siberia. After an attempted escape, she was given another four year sentence. In 1903, during a brief "free period" she visited several city governments in Russia, collecting evidence of the Tsar's repression. Jailed again in 1908, her final release did not come until 1917 when Kerensky freed her after the February Revolution. Her sympathies were not totally with the new regime's politics, however, and she exiled herself to Prague. By the time she died, she had spent forty-four of her seventy-three years as a political prisoner. Her letters and memoirs were edited by Alice Stone Blackwell (Lucy Stone's daughter) and she wrote her autobiography, HIDDEN SPRINGS OF THE RUSSIAN REVOLUTION in 1931.

"Catherine Breshkovskaya" LECTURES ON WOMEN OF THE MODERN WORLD. Scripps College Papers No. 6, Scripps College, California: March 1936, p. 64

SOFYA PEROVSKAYA
1853-1881
"First woman in Russia to be executed for a political act"

On Feb. 19, 1861, Tsar Alexander II abolished serfdom and along with it came some changes for long-oppressed women. Universities began to open up. Student became synonymous with Revolutionary and as the Tsar gave a little they asked for more. In 1874, the "Chaykovtsi" was formed—a group of socialists, anarchists ad student intellectuals eager to put theory into practice. In response to the intellectual radicals of the period, Bakunin and Marx, the students were beginning to leave the universities to work with the farmers, whom Bakunin said had a "special strength and knowledge" to transmit to their privileged intellectual comrades. Perovskaya was a leading member of the "Chaykovtsi;" "tenacious, silent, fearless and self-possessed, the comrades submitted to her strong will, her experience, and her acknowledged authority in the most important undertakings."[1] The daughter of a wealthy Russian landowner, she'd been beaten and bullied by her father and had left home as soon as possible to attend university, where she joined the revolutionaries. Arrested for advocating social revolution among villagers with whom she was working as a teacher and health worker, she was sent to Siberia. She escaped on the way, and returned to St. Petersburg to continue organizing. On May 1, 1881, Tsar Alexander II was assassinated on her order. She had brought the bomb to the spot, prepared and planned the action and gave the decisive order at the right moment. Sofya was arrested and hanged for this political act, by those whose purposes it foiled, and revered as a martyr by those thousands it liberated.

1. Halle, Fannina, WOMEN IN SOVIET RUSSIA, p. 56-57
Halle, Fannina, WOMEN IN SOVIET RUSSIA. N.Y.: Viking Press, 1933

MARY LEASE
1853-1933/Agrarian Reformer & Feminist

"The Kansas Pythoness" as she was known, studied law in 1885 in Wichita, Kansas and was admitted to the bar. In 1888, needing income and a creative outlet for her energies, she became involved in the Populist Movement for agrarian reform. She was an effective and bold speaker and after addressing a State Convention of the Union Labor Party in Kansas, was nominated for county office even though she, as a woman, couldn't vote. She was defeated, but she continued stumping for the Populists, and in Georgia said: "You may call me an anarchist, a socialist or a communist, I care not, but I hold to the theory that if one man has not enough to eat three times a day and another man has twenty-five million dollars, that last man has something that belongs to the first."[1] The Populists disappeared after 1895, absorbed into the Democratic

Party, and the "Kansas Pythoness" went to New York City to write for the "World." In 1895, she published THE PROBLEM OF CIVILIZATION SOLVED; bold in scope, it advocated woman suffrage, prohibition, evolution, and birth control; a book far ahead of its time.

1. Johnson, Gerald, LUNATIC FRINGE, p. 163
Johnson, Gerald, THE LUNATIC FRINGE, N.Y.: Lippincott Co., 1957, p. 158ff

ROSA LUXEMBURG
1871-1919/Revolutionary

At the age of nineteen, she fled her native Poland under threat of arrest as a political activist, went to Switzerland to study socialist writers, and earned her doctorate at Zurich with a thesis on the economic history of Poland. For more than twenty years, she lived with a Polish revolutionary—she as theoretician and propagandist and he as the organizer. Her commitment to the revolutionary life did not come without struggle, and she frequently lamented the fact that she could not settle down and have a family. In 1898, she moved to Berlin (arranging a marriage of convenience to a German, to gain a residence permit) and joined the largest and most prestigious socialist party, the German Social Democrats (SPD). Her stay in the SPD was stormy; she battled with "revisionists" who sought revolutionary change through "reform" and election victories. Rosa wrote pamphlets and spoke in support of traditional Marxist theories of revolution. She was committed to developing class consciousness in all with no elite and no leaders. She advocated the general strike as a powerful revolutionary tool, and spoke against splintering within the party (but was often one of the splinters). In 1914, when the SPD representatives in the Reichstag voted for war appropriations, she and Lenin were among the few socialists who opposed the war and she was jailed. At this time, she and Karl Liebknecht founded the Spartacist Party—considered the most radical wing of the SPD, and it later became the German Communist Party. She was released from jail in 1918 having written a controversial pamphlet called "Crisis in German Social Democracy," in which she denounced socialist support of the capitalist-imperialist war. She also wrote a paper criticizing some aspects of the Russian Revolution of 1917, and these kind of writings encouraged free debate between socialists, although they were not totally welcome, since many of her comrades preferred her to follow the party line. On Jan. 13, 1919, she and Liebknecht were captured by troops of the Freikorps (counter-revolutionaries), and the socialist government made up of the most "reform" segment of the SPD, did not help her because she was a Spartacist, too radical and too dangerous. She and Liebknecht were bludgeoned with rifle butts and shot. Her body was dumped in the Landwehr canal and not found until the following May. During her lifetime she had written over 700 books, articles and pamphlets, all defining, questioning and criticizing the political climate of her day.

Whitman, Karen, "Rosa Luxemburg" WOMEN: A JOURNAL OF LIBERA-TION, Summer, 1970, p. 16

Frolich, Paul, ROSA LUXEMBURG (1940) [see p. 28 for portrait]

ANGELICA BALABANOFF
1878-1965/Russian Revolutionary

Born into a wealthy family and trained to be a "lady" she had to fight all kinds of conditioning to arrive at her socialist beliefs. As a child, she'd been forced to accompany her mother on charitable relief trips, and was horrified by the poverty she saw on one end and the affluence in her own home. At eleven, Angelica won a battle to be allowed to go to school with the "peasants" and taught herself Russian (she'd been allowed to learn only foreign languages in her parents' efforts to make her a woman of "quality."). At nineteen, she went to Brussels to University. And there Balabanoff got her doctorate and in 1900 joined the Socialist party of Italy. Here, she worked closely with Lenin, but frequently found herself at odds with him. She argued for unity and he for splintering as many times as it took to get a "pure" party. He was, to her mind, partisan, factional and authoritarian, and she, democratic and humanitarian. Despite these differences, Angelica worked with Lenin from 1915-21 and they were drawn together by opposition to World War I and their enthusiasm for the Russian Revolution of 1917. She split when she saw old socialists imprisoned in the Tsar's prisons for dissent against, not the Tsar, but the new Bolshevik regime. Seeing Bolsheviks slaughter the sailor revolutionaries at Kronstadt and perceiving Lenin to be in the business of bribing all those he couldn't convince through action or word was too much for her. She managed to break with the party without being personally slandered and considered herself one of the few who actually accomplished this.

Balabanoff, Angelica, IMPRESSIONS OF LENIN, Michigan: Univ. of Mich. Press, 1968 [see p. 28 for portrait]

CONSTANCE MARKIEVICZ
1876-1927/Irish Revolutionist

She began as an aristocrat bored by high society. In 1897, she went to avant-garde Paris to study art and there she married a Polish nobleman. They settled in Dublin in 1900 and both became leaders of a young artistic and literary circle. There their similarities ended. She became involved in the struggle for Irish Independence and estranged from the Count who did not approve of either the struggle or a woman's involvement in it. Constance first came into national prominence in 1908 with her vocal support for bar maids, whose work had been drastically altered by new liquor licensing laws, and in 1913, she supported a labor strike and ran a soup kitchen for strikers' families. Shortly thereafter, she became a Sinn Fein leader. This group, devoted to Irish Independence, made her a commander and she lead 120 rebels during the Easter Rebellion of 1916 in Dublin. Besieged by British troops, she was the last of the Sinn Fein leaders to surrender. Tried for treason the same year, she was given a death sentence which was commuted to life imprisonment. She was released during the amnesty of 1917, only to be arrested again in 1918 and jailed. Markievicz became the first woman to win election to the British House of Commons but refused to serve until Ireland was free. In 1919 she was appointed minister of labor in Eamon de Valera's cabinet and remained active in Irish politics for several years. She was called the "Red Countess" by her enemies and "Irish Joan of Arc" by her friends. Her biography has been written by Sean O'Faolain, CONSTANCE MARKIEVICZ: OR THE AVERAGE REVOLUTIONARY, and her prison letters were published in Toronto in 1934, edited by Eva Gore-Booth. [see p. 28 for portrait]

MARGARET SANGER
1879-1966/Birth Control Pioneer

The credo of Sanger's journal "The Woman Rebel" (set up in 1914 to publicize the birth control issues) was the credo of her life: "to look the world in the face with a go-to-hell look in the eyes; to have an idea; to speak and act in defiance of convention,"[1] and so she did. Around the turn of the century, she decided to study nursing and in the course of her work saw hundreds of women give birth under the most deplorable of conditions. This experience convinced her that the one impediment to world peace and happiness and sexual equality was overpopulation. For several years she tried to solve the problem through work with the socialists and her home became a center where the "greats" of American socialism gathered: Goldman, Steffens, Haywood, et. al. She wrote a column for their magazine, "The Call," entitled "What Every Girl Should Know," (on female health problems) and gave health talks to working women. Over and over these women asked about contraception. Determined to find an answer, she traveled to Europe, read any books that vaguely related to the topic, studied and asked questions. Finally, under indictment on an obscenity charge (from an issue of the "Woman Rebel") she wrote "Family Limitation," a pamphlet about birth control. "Overnight, the name Margaret Sanger became synonymous with a challenge to the law."[2] She was committed to being the standard bearer. When she discovered that the Dutch had perfected an efficient form of birth control, the diaphragm, Sanger, with customary speed and efficiency, set about introducing it into the USA and challenging all hindering laws. She set up a clinic in Brownsville in New York City and was promptly arrested along with her sister, and given thirty days. After her release, she wrote, lectured, and hunted for better contraceptive methods. She published WOMAN AND THE NEW RACE dealing with women in labor and updated her pamphlet on family limitation. With some funds from her new husband, 3-in-one oil tycoon, Noah Slee, Sanger set up the Clinical Research Bureau (CRB), the organization which eventually effected a change in the laws against distribution of contraceptive information. She organized conferences in the US and Europe and gathered support for the cause for the next decade. Arrested several times, she never had to spend much time in jail because public support from writers, churches (except the Catholic Church) and women's clubs was loud and powerful. In the early fifties, she saw her final goal realized: the International Planned Parenthood organization was founded—a group to carry on on a global scale. When the pill was finally a reality and millions of women had comprehensive, reliable contraception, she rested. She died at 87, knowing that her work had radically changed not only the present but also the future.

1. *Taft-Douglas, Emily, MARGARET SANGER: PIONEER OF THE FUTURE, p. 50*
2. *Taft-Douglas, Emily, p. 57*
Taft-Douglas, Emily, MARGARET SANGER: PIONEER OF THE FUTURE. New York: Holt, Rinehart and Winston, 1970
Stoddard, Hope, "Margaret Sanger" FAMOUS AMERICAN WOMEN, N.Y.: Thomas Y. Crowell, Co., 1970, p. 372   [see p. 28 for portrait]

ELIZABETH GURLEY FLYNN
1890-1964/Union Organizer, "The Rebel Girl"

She began her career as a socialist union organizer in 1906 at the Harlem Socialist Club. She was not quite 16 and she gave a speech called "What Socialism Will do for Women." It was such a success that she dropped out of high school and devoted herself to the cause, and in 1907 was the only female delegate present at the 3rd Convention of the IWW (Industrial Workers of the World), the Wobblies. In 1908, she was inspired to continue organizing by meeting "Mother Mary" Jones, whom she called the "greatest woman agitator of our time." She married at 17 but never lived with her husband more than a few months—quickly choosing politics over housework. When arrested in Spokane, Washington, for "conspiracy to incite men to violate the law," she was horrified by the conditions of the women's jails. Her outspoken agitation brought about matrons in county jails in Spokane (there had previously been only male guards). She was acquitted because of lack of evidence and "ill health" (her pregnancy). In 1913, she met Carlo Tresca, an Italian anarchist and lived openly with him for the next 13 years. She was a prime organizer of women during the Lawrence, Massachusetts, textile strike (of "bread and roses" fame) in 1912 and from Lawrence she moved on to aid strikes in New Bedford, Lowell, Mass., and New York City, where she organized a hotel waiters' strike. The war years, 1914-1919 were filled with bloody repression of Wobblies and from 1917 the IWW became a defense organization dedicated to freeing its members from jails. At 26, Flynn devoted herself to this work and never again did formal organizing. She is one of the founders of the American Civil Liberties Union (which later expelled her) and in 1937 joined the Communist Party, becoming the first woman chairman (sic) in 1961. In 1951 she was arrested under the Smith Act and at 63 went to jail for "teaching and advocating the violent overthrow of the government." She was in and out of the Women's House of Detention in New York from 1951-55 (mostly for contempt of court sentences of 30 days each) but in 1955 was sent to Alderson, the federal prison for women in West Virginia to serve a three year sentence. She said of this experience: "Come what may, I was a political prisoner, and proud of it . . . I felt no shame, no humiliation, no consciousness of guilt. To me my number, 11710, was a badge of honor."[1]

1. Gurley-Flynn, E. THE ALDERSON STORY, p. 29
Gurley-Flynn, E. THE ALDERSON STORY, New York: International Publ., 1963
Hoke, Mardon, "The Rebel Girl" WOMEN: A JOURNAL OF LIBERATION, Spring, 1970, p. 25   [see p. 28 for portrait]

DOLORES IBARRURI
1895- /La Pasionaria

On the day the fascists rebelled against the democratic Spanish Republic, July 18, 1936, La Pasionaria said on Madrid radio: "It is better to die on your feet than to live on your knees," a rallying cry for all who wanted to make Spain the grave of fascism. Born in poverty in Basque country, she and her Austrian miner husband lived on his meager income, working together politically in strikes but barely surviving physically. Eventually, she rebelled against domestic drudgery and endless poverty and turned to communism and socialism. It was a difficult decision—years of Catholicism had imbued her with the sense that poverty was a personal failure rather than a social condition that could be remedied by political aciton. She protested the position of women: "I rebelled against the idea that we were condemned to drage the shackles of poverty and submission through the centuries like beasts of burden, slapped, beaten, ground down by the men chosen to be our life companions."[1] By 1931, with the establishment of the New Republic, she was working full time for the Communist Party in Madrid as editor of "Mundo Obrero" (Worker's World) and also in charge of women's activities in the Politburo. This same year she was arrested for the first time (for being a Communist Party member) and while in prison lectured on the party, and refused to cooperate with authorities. Several arrests and jail sentences of varying duration followed. In 1936, the Popular Front was formed; it was a union of socialists, communists and republicans, and that same year a military coup lead by General Franco started the Civil War. She helped to build the united fronts against fascism and made numerous radio broadcasts pleading the front's cause. Spain was not the grave of fascism, but La Pasionaria did all she could to make it so.

1. Ibarruri, Dolores, *THEY SHALL NOT PASS, p. 61*
Ibarruri, Dolores, THEY SHALL NOT PASS, N.Y.: International Pub., 1966 [see p. 28 for portrait]

FADELA M'RABET
Algerian Feminist

Director of the "women's hour" on Radio Algiers and, as a feminist, she has written a scathing attack on men and the social atmosphere of Algeria—protesting the treatment of women as objects—sexual, political and economic, called LA FEMME AL-GERIENNE.

Gordon, David, WOMEN OF ALGERIA: AN ESSAY ON CHANGE

MRS. HUDA SHARAWI
Pioneer Egyptian Feminist

She went as a delegate to a conference on women in Rome and upon her return, threw her veil into the sea, marking the beginning of active feminism in Egypt—1923.

Gordon, David, WOMEN OF ALGERIA: AN ESSAY ON CHANGE

See Also: Abigail Adams, Lucretia Mott, Frances Wright, Leila Mahmedbekova, Prudence Crandall

Educators

COMTESSE GENLIS
1746-1830/Educational Progressive

As a teacher, she was two hundred years ahead of her time. She evolved ingenious and progressive theories of education which made learning a pleasure; for example: teaching history via magic lantern slides, teaching botany by having her pupils go on walks in the woods with a botanist, and writing her own texts, some of which were short comedies her students could act out. As a sideline, she wrote historical novels and romances!

Adelman, Joseph, "Comtesse Genlis," FAMOUS WOMEN, New York: Ellis Lonow, Co., 1926, p. 113

LUCY LARCOM
1826-1893/Mill worker, Poet & Teacher

As an adolescent, Lucy Larcom worked in the notorious Lowell, Massachusetts cotton mills, and contributed regularly to the mill-workers' literary journal, LOWELL OFFERING. She and the other workers met in a reading club where they read, discussed and presented papers. At twenty, she began teaching school in Illinois, and from there went to work at the Monticello Female Seminary. From 1854-62, she taught at Wheaton Female Seminary (now Wheaton College) and she eventually became editor of a magazine called "Our Young Folks." Larcom published several books of poetry: SIMILITUDES (1854), POEMS (1869), and CHILDHOOD SONGS (1873). She published an autobiography in 1899 called NEW ENGLAND GIRLHOOD.

PRUDENCE CRANDALL
1803-1889

Crandall blazed new trails in the field of education for Black women. In 1833 she opened a school for Black girls in Canterbury, Connecticut, and the hostile community galvanized itself into action. Public meetings were convened, committees of wealthy townsfolk called on her, village meetings denounced the school in racist resolutions, and those who spoke in her support were bullied and threatened into silence. The villagers threw aside all restraint on her opening day and began unconditional and violent attacks using any tactic they could conceive of to destroy her institution and "idea" that Blacks should be educated. Stores refused to provide her with food, medicine or supplies. The village doctor refused to treat her students, pupils were insulted in the streets and the school building and her house were smeared with filth, and manure poured down her well. Not satisfied with harrassment and beligerance, the townsfolk pressed for a new law—passed by the legislature on May 24, 1833, called the "Black Law." This forbade the establishment of any school for the instruction of "colored persons" not inhabitants of Connecticut. Crandall was arrested on June 27 for breaking the law (her students came from New York, Boston and Philadelphia). Those who rallied to her support formed a paper called "The Unionist" to publicize the case and the Connecticut Female Anti-Slavery Society was formed for her support. She spent a night in jail and was bailed out. Tried twice, she was acquitted on a technicality, in July, 1834. The cost of the litigation was such that the school had to close for lack of funds. The bigots had won—at least on the surface. But several of her pupils did go on to become teachers and ardent abolitionists, so in the long run the bigots were defeated and Crandall's far-reaching vision and courageous fortitude had tangible results for years. She was voted a pension (primarily due to the efforts on her behalf of Mark Twain) by the Connecticut legislature, but she lived to collect it only six years.

Katz, William, "Prejudice Destroys a School in Connecticut," EYEWIT-NESS: THE NEGRO IN AMERICAN HISTORY, N.Y.: Pitman Pub. Corp., 1968, p. 151-53
Sillen, Samuel, "Prudence Crandall," WOMEN AGAINST SLAVERY, N.Y.: Masses & Mainstream, 1955, p. 11ff [see p. 43 for portrait]

MARY McCLEOD BETHUNE
1875-1955

It wasn't easy to get an education in the late 1800's if you were Black *and* a woman *and* one of seventeen children, but Bethune did. After high school and Moody Bible Institute, she was assigned to Haines Normal School in Augusta, Georgia, as a teacher. She had planned to be a missionary to Africa, but the Missionary Board turned her down because she was Black. She wasn't happy about being based in the heart of Ku Klux Klan country, but "resigned" herself to working with fellow Black Americans, and discovered that the task of providing education for her oppressed brothers and sisters was as large if not larger than all the problems of Africa. For the next several years, she worked at various schools in the South, got married, had a child, did prison reform work and began thinking about an "impossible dream"—a school of her own. She hunted for buildings and land outside Daytona, Florida, and rented (on credit) a four room house. She then scavenged equipment and furniture from the garbage piles of hotels and the town dump, and in 1904, opened the Daytona Education and Industrial Training School for Negro Girls. She charged $.50 a week to those who could afford it and began to teach the girls "to earn a living." With prodigious courage and strength, she began the search for funds to keep it going: "I rang doorbells and tackled cold prospects without a lead. I wrote articles for whoever would print them, distributed leaflets, rode interminable miles of dusty roads on my old bicycle, invaded churches, clubs, lodges, chambers of commerce."[1] By 1925, her school became the Cookman Collegiate, later Bethune-Cookman College. In 1933, Roosevelt made her Director of the Division of Negro Affairs in the newly formed National Youth Administration, and she was able, through this position, to open up jobs for hundreds of Black men and women. In 1935, she organized the National Council of Negro Women, whose membership represented almost all the Negro women's clubs in the country.

1. Bowie, Walter, WOMEN OF LIGHT, p. 124

Bowie, Walter, "Mary Bethune" WOMEN OF LIGHT, N.Y.: Harper & Row, 1963, p. 119f

Daniel, Sadie, I. "Mary Bethune" WOMEN BUILDERS, Washington D.C.: The Associated Pub., 1931, p. 79f

Stoddard, Hope, "Mary Bethune" FAMOUS AMERICAN WOMEN, N.Y.: Thomas Y. Crowell, Co., 1970, p. 71f   [see cover for portrait]

See also: Annie Peck, Florence Nightingale, Philippa of Hainault

◀Dr. Mary Walker
Florence Nightingale▶

Mary Somerville
▼

Scientists and Inventors

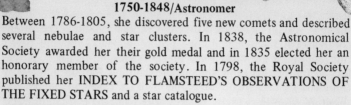

CAROLINE HERSCHEL
1750-1848/Astronomer

Between 1786-1805, she discovered five new comets and described several nebulae and star clusters. In 1838, the Astronomical Society awarded her their gold medal and in 1835 elected her an honorary member of the society. In 1798, the Royal Society published her INDEX TO FLAMSTEED'S OBSERVATIONS OF THE FIXED STARS and a star catalogue.

Adelman, Joseph, FAMOUS WOMEN, p. 114

MARY SOMERVILLE
1780-1872/Scientist

Mary Somerville experimented on the magnetic influence of violet rays in the solar spectrum and her results were published in "Philosophical Transactions" of 1826. In 1827, the "whole character and course" of her life changed (as she put it). She was asked to do a translation of LaPlace's MECANIQUE CÉLESTE (about the structure of the universe) and it was an instant success when published in 1831 as MECHANISM OF THE HEAVENS. In 1834, she published "The Connection of the Physical Sciences" and "Physical Geography" and as a result was given a pension by the King of £ 300 a year. In the 1860's, she took an active part in women's rights activities and signed a petition presented to the University of London asking that women sit for degree exams. She was also a member of the General Committee for Woman Suffrage in London. Her last work was "Molecular and Microscopic Science," a summary of recent discoveries in chemistry and physics, and in 1869, she received the Victoria Medal of the Royal Geographical Society and was made an honorary member of the Royal Astronomical Society. "The greatest scientists of her day saw in her, their peer."[1]

1. Stenton, Doris, ENGLISH WOMAN IN HISTORY, p. 332
Stenton, Doris, ENGLISH WOMAN IN HISTORY, London: George Allen & Unwin, Ltd., 1957, p. 329ff
Adelman, Joseph, FAMOUS WOMEN, p. 123   [see above for portrait]

MARIA MITCHELL
1818-1889/Astronomer

Mitchell was awarded many honors, perhaps the most pivotal being the gold medal offered by the King of Denmark for the first person to discover a comet through a telescope—she did so in 1847 and it made her famous. When Vassar opened in 1865, she was invited to join the faculty and taught astronomy in a new and different way for the next twenty-three years. She refused to grade, feeling you couldn't judge a human mind in terms of a letter grade, and taught her subject with such verve and vividness her pupils thought nothing of getting up in the middle of the night to troop up to the roof and catch sight of an infrequently seen astral phenomenon. When Matthew Vassar died in 1868, women faculty were discriminated against—left off committees, given less pay, and not allowed to lecture off campus. Mitchell challenged the latter and spoke all over the United States, and not just on astronomy. She felt strongly about astronomy, but more strongly about the position of women—and she spoke out about it. She was elected president of the Association for the Advancement of Women in 1874, and was the first woman admitted to the American Academy of Arts & Sciences and the Association for the Advancement of Science. In addition, her name is carved on the front of the Boston Public Library as a "great American;" she has also received an honorary doctorate from Columbia, and perhaps most dramatically, has had a crater named after her on the moon!

Stoddard, Hope, "Maria Mitchell" FAMOUS AMERICAN WOMEN, NY: Thomas Y. Crowell Co., 1970, p. 295

Kendall, Phebe Mitchell (ed.) MARIA MITCHELL, LIFE, LETTERS AND JOURNALS (Lee & Shepard 1896)

Wright, Helen, SWEEPER IN THE SKY: THE LIFE OF MARIA MITCHELL, FIRST WOMEN ASTRONOMER IN AMERICA, NY: Macmillan Co., 1949 [see cover for portrait]

FLORENCE NIGHTINGALE
1820-1910/Founder of Modern Nursing

Education and the care of the sick were really the only two fields open to women in the 19th Century and the former became formalized with the opening of teachers' colleges for women and the latter when Nightingale opened a school for nursing and elevated the profession to a "fine art," in her words. She began her career in 1851 when she took over a sanatorium for infirm and ailing governesses and made it an efficient and healthy place. Her genius for administration was dazzlingly displayed when she organized a hospital unit of 38 nurses for the Crimean War in 1854. This war was more than usually bloody and was killing hundreds of men a day, not just from casualties on the field but from infection, and lack of care in unsanitary battlefront hospitals. She saved hundreds of lives, changing the death rate during that year from 41/100 to 2/100. She introduced standardized training, sanitary reforms, and over much opposition, gained needed supplies on the battlefront. She convinced doctors of the pressing need for "follow-up" care of patients and the need to have consistently efficiently run, nurse-staffed hospitals. In 1860, she founded the Nightingale School & Home for Training Nurses in London. The "Lady of the Lamp" was the first woman to receive the British Order of Merit (1907) and is the subject of Longfellow's poem, "Santa Filomena."

Adelman, Joseph, FAMOUS WOMEN, p. 156 [see p. 46 for portrait]

DR. MARY WALKER
1832-1919/Surgeon

She graduated as a doctor at the age of 23 and at 29 entered the Union Army as an Assistant Surgeon with the rank of First Lieutenant. She wanted to dress according to her rank and so adopted clothes like her fellow officers. She challenged the army on this point and a special act of Congress gave her official permission to dress as she pleased. After the war, she maintained her male garb and is the only woman in America to have her rights of dress protected by national legislation. She earned a living by lecturing and writing and occasionally practiced medicine, although few would patronize her because of her "eccentric habits." She was also the only woman to receive the Congressional Medal of Honor. But her name was removed from the list of winners in 1917 for "undisclosed reasons."

Adelman, Joseph, FAMOUS WOMEN, p. 204 [see p. 46 for portrait]

See Also: Edith Cavell

Louisa May Alcott
Writer & Feminist

Victoria Woodhull, Journalist
(Among Many Other Things!)

George Sand
Novelist

Writers, Journalists and Printers

APHRA BEHN

1640-1689/"First Englishwoman to earn her living as a writer"

She is credited by some, as the "inventor of the novel with a purpose," and the first advocate of a "cause" in fiction. While living with her family in Guiana, she wrote the story of the African slave and chief, who was her friend and companion there. OROONOK was an exposure of the crimes of slavery, and wasn't published until a year before her death. When she returned to England between 1658 and 1664, she was asked to give an account to the King (Charles II) of the state of British Guiana, and because of the professionalism of her report and her knowledge of Dutch, she was asked to be a political spy in Antwerp after her husband's death in 1665. The British were at war with the Dutch from 1665-67 and wanted to keep an eye on the Dutch fleet's movements. She did so, and received no pay, returning to England destitute and seeking remuneration. No one would pay her bills, let alone reimburse her for her work, so she was sent to debtor's prison! Eventually a kind friend paid her debts and she was released, vowing never to work for the state again. In 1670, she decided to make a living with her pen and wrote several plays, most were comedies and almost all were popular. She wrote 18 novels in all and lived well from her royalties. In 1682, Aphra Behn ceased writing plays (possibly because of political pressure—her satires were candid and biting) and turned to poetry. In 1684, she published her first volume, full of descriptions of passionate love. As Virginia Woolf said: "All women together ought to let flowers fall on the tomb of Aphra Behn, for it was she who earned them the right to speak their minds." (from A ROOM OF ONE'S OWN)

Sackville-West, Victoria, APHRA BEHN: THE INCOMPARABLE ASTREA, New York: Viking Press, 1928

Behn, Aphra, SELECTED WRITINGS OF THE INGENIOUS MRS. APHRA BEHN, New York: Grove Press, 1950 [see cover for portrait]

ANN FRANKLIN
1696-1763/Printer & Journalist

After her husband's death in 1735, Ann Franklin (sister-in-law of Ben Franklin) took over his printing business and made it thrive. She did blanks for public offices, printed pamphlets and money, and in 1740, did an edition of the the laws of Rhode Island. Her son started the first paper in Rhode Island, the "Newport Mercury" and at his death in 1762, she took it over also, and ran it profitably until her death one year later.

Dexter, Elisabeth, COLONIAL WOMEN OF AFFAIRS, Boston: Houghton-Mifflin, 1931

GEORGE SAND
1804-1876/Novelist

Born Aurore Dupin, she married the Baron Dudevant for "convenience" (more his than hers) and formally divorced him in 1836. Before the divorce, she went to Paris to live with Jules Sandeau (whose shortened last name provided her with a pseudonym). In 1832, her first novel INDIANA was published, and excited much criticism because of its "radical" views on social questions. Sand usually worked out her own problems in her novels and hers were controversial ones. Although her life is peppered with male lovers, she maintained a close and loving relationship with Marie Dorval, which like Christina of Sweden's relationship with Belle Sparre, was openly affectionate and demonstrative. For the next forty years, she lived pretty much as she pleased in a chateau with her son Maurice; she entertained, wrote (one-hundred-twenty volumes in all) and carried on a lively correspondence with the novelists, poets, and celebrities of the day—Flaubert, de Musset, Chopin, Balzac, Dumas and so forth. Politically, she called herself a Communist, but her pacifism and religious bent made her a strange breed of revolutionary to her friends. What she wanted was an end to poverty and a universal sharing of natural resources—which was closer to the Communist point of view than any other she could find at the time. She was not, strictly speaking, a feminist, but she did feel that women should have equality with men, in laws and love. She despised the marriage laws, the double standard, and punitive laws against women adulterers were particularly abhorrent to her. On the other hand, however, she believed firmly in the "duties of motherhood," and did not feel "mothering" and political office mixed. All her life, people had been wavering in their treatment of George Sand—what sex role did she play? She herself gave ambivalent and ambiguous cues. After her death Flaubert expressed it in a letter to Turgenief: "Poor dear, great, woman! Only those who knew her as I did can realize just how much of the feminine there was in that great man, how deep the tenderness which was so integral a part of her genius . . . "[1]

1. Maurois, Andre, p. 463

Marois, Andre, LELIA, NY: Harper & Bros., 1954

deMorny, Peter, THE BEST YEARS OF THEIR LIVES, London: Centaur Press, Lmt., 1955, p. 171 [see p. 49 for portrait]

LOUISA MAY ALCOTT
1832-1888/ Writer & Feminist

Alcott's childhood was hardly traditional; her father was considered a "freak" because he was an idealist and Transcendentalist, and the family moved constantly as he sought meaningful employment. This had the happy result of bringing Louisa in contact with progressive ideas, and gave her an unusual amount of freedom from artificial role restrictions. When her family moved to Concord, Massachusetts, so her father could be near the leaders of the Transcendentalist movement, Louisa began composing dramas and stories for her friends. Emerson became her mentor and close adult friend, and it was for his daughter, Ellen, she began telling the stories that comprised her first book, FLOWER FABLES (Published in 1854). Soon she was selling stories regularly, for $5 and $10 apiece, and decided to try to make a living writing. To pay the debts not covered by her writing, she did sewing, acted as a governess, and read to the elderly. In 1860, she really began to "make it" as a writer and sold a story to the "Atlantic Monthly" for $50. By 1864, she was making $600 a year and when LITTLE WOMEN was published in 1868, she was deemed an "author" (sic.). "Everyone read it, lawyers . . . commuters . . . wives . . . and of course young ladies . . . "[1] It paid all the Alcott family debts and provided some measure of luxury. Books followed in swift succession: 1870–LITTLE MEN, 1876–ROSE IN BLOOM, 1877–UNDER THE LILACS. All were successful and by 1888, her earnings amounted to $8000 in six months! Eight years before her death, 1880, she became interested in the Women's Rights Movement and wrote to a friend: "Let us hear no more of 'woman's sphere' from the State House or pulpit—no more twaddle about sturdy oaks and clinging vines. Let woman find out her own limitations, but in heaven's name, give her a chance! Let the professions be opened to her. Let fifty years of college education be hers. And then we shall see what she can do!"[2] Although she had been able to overcome the restrictions imposed on her by a sexist 19th Century society to the extent that she could earn a living doing something she liked, she remembered to speak out for her less fortunate sisters and to call for reform so that they too could "make it."

1. Stoddard, Hope, "L.M. Alcott" FAMOUS AMERICAN WOMEN, p. 21
2. Stoddard, Hope, p. 22
Stoddard, Hope, "L.M. Alcott," FAMOUS AMERICAN WOMEN, N.Y.: Thomas Y. Crowell Co., 1970, p. 12ff
King, William, "L.M. Alcott" WOMAN, Springfield, Mass: The King-Richardson Co., 1900, p. 410 [see p. 49 for portrait]

VICTORIA WOODHULL
1838-1927/Journalist (among many other things!)

She challenged every single convention existing in the 19th Century! She was a spiritualist who really believed she could reach a control named Demosthenes, and she and her family made a living as a traveling side show offering elixirs, spiritualism and patent medicines. She married Woodhull and brought him into *her* family rather than going into his, and had a son, and daughter (whom she named Zulu Maude!). When she divorced him, he became a drug addict and a skid row bum, and when she took him back into her care, in sympathy (she was then living with another man) she was constantly maligned for maintaining a "menage a trois." Well aware of the oppressive atmosphere of her society, she decided that no woman could get what she wanted without grabbing for it with all she had. She and her sister Tennessee wheedled some money out of a wealthy tycoon and set up their own brokerage firm on all male Wall Street. They made enough money to finance their next adventure, WOODHULL & CLAF-LIN'S WEEKLY, a muckraking journal devoted to all the controversial issues of the day. Within its pages she editorialized in favor of free love (as better than legal marriage to a man you despise), woman suffrage, abolition of the death penalty, birth control, occultism, legal prostitution and in addition, the sisters published the first full version in English of the Communist Manifesto! In addition, Victoria used the "Weekly" to push her own candidacy for the presidency. She wanted very much to represent the suffragists but alienated her friends Susan Anthony and E.C. Stanton by her high-handed attempts to nominate herself (on their behalf) without asking them. Having lost their support, she created the Equal Rights Party and nominated herself and Frederick Douglass as vice-president (which he declined) in 1872. She was in jail on an obscenity charge when U.S. Grant beat her! By 1877, she and Tennessee had just about exhausted the possibilities for action and income in America and went to England to marry rich noblemen. Tennessee did and became a Baroness, and Victoria married a rich and prominent banker. She ran again for president by mail, in 1892, and died at 90 in her country estate, well respected and considered a "genteel old lady!"

Johnson, Gerald, "Victoria Woodhull," THE LUNATIC FRINGE, NY: Lippincott, Co., 1957, p. 80ff
Wallace, Irving, "Victoria Woodhull" THE SQUARE PEGS, N.Y.: Alfred Knopf, 1957, p. 100 [see p. 49 for portrait]

GABRIELA MISTRAL
1899-1957/ Chilean Poet, Winner of Nobel Prize in Literature

Lucila Godoy Alcayaga (who adopted the pseudonym Gabriela Mistral after Gabriele D'Annunzio of Italy and Frédéric Mistral of France, both poets), taught secondary school from 1912 to 1918. She quickly rose to "prominent and important posts" in the Chilean educational system, and in 1922, she went to Mexico and reorganized the rural schools of that country. From 1926 to 1939 she represented her country on the Committee of Arts and Letters of the League of Nations and as Chilean consul at Lisbon, Madrid, Nice and Los Angeles. As an internationally recognized poet

(Nobel Prize in Literature, l945), Mistral taught at the Universities of Puerto Rico, Montevideo, and at Barnard, Middlebury and Vassar in the United States. Her poetry has been described as "mystic," "religious, direct and uncluttered;" it has been widely published and translated.

TAJIKHAN SHADIYEVA
Editor and Soviet-Turkish Feminist

There were no organizations for women in Uzbekistan (Soviet Turkey) until the 1920's. After centuries of the most incredibly oppressive patriarchy, women's clubs were formed and these led the struggle for women's liberation in the Soviet East. Tajikhan Shadiyeva was a "brilliant organizer and burning firebrand"[1] in this movement. At the age of 11 she was sold for 200 roubles to a man who'd had nine wives, one of whom he had murdered with impunity. He beat Tajikhan, bullied her and strictly enforced the wearing of a veil. After the Revolution in Russia, she managed to learn how to read and write (thanks to the revolutionaries who organized in her community). This was enough of a taste of the possibilities of future freedom to raise her expectations; but reality became more intolerable. She attempted suicide once, but was saved, and that ended her submission. She had tried to turn her frustration, rage and passion on herself, now she turned it on the struggle against patriarchy. She left her husband and went to university, where she received first prize (in Moscow) for her thesis: "The Crisis in the Capitalist Countries" and at 30 became a member of the government of the Federal Republic of Uzbekistan. Perhaps her most influential role has been as editor of the largest Uzbeck Women's journal—Yengi Yul (The New Road) from whose pages she has editorialized about the rights of women to free bodies and free minds.

1. *Green, Margaret, WOMEN IN THE SOVIET EAST, p. 313*
Green, Margaret, WOMEN IN THE SOVIET EAST, New York: Dutton & Co., Inc., 1938

See Also: Comtesse Genlis, Lucy Larcom, Mercy Warren, Jane G. Swisshelm, Mary Lease, Rosa Luxemburg, Margaret Sanger, Fadela M'Rabet, Louise Labé, Mary Wollstonecraft, Sojourner Truth, Caroline Norton, Margaret Fuller, Emily Faithful, Sarojini Naidu

◀ Sarah Bernhardt
(as Hamlet)

Entertainers

CHARLOTTE CUSHMAN
1816-1878/Actress

HARRIET HOSMER
1830-1908/Sculptor

Cushman made her debut as an actress in 1845 and played Hamlet, Romeo and over ten other male leads in addition to the predictable female roles. She had an unusual power to attract the passionate feelings of other women and her biographies are peppered with references to the intense feeling women friends had for her. Gamaliel Bradford (BIOGRAPHY AND THE HUMAN HEART, Boston: Houghton Mifflin, 1932) says: "... there is a virile element in her, which she strove neither to diminish or conceal."[1] The same author also describes her as a tomboy, a life-long lover of sports not considered feminine, and is convinced Cushman wished to be a man. Charlotte and Harriet Hosmer lived together or near each other for several years. Hosmer was the daughter of a doctor who raised her as a boy, encouraging her interest in becoming a doctor. This scheme was later abandoned in favor of art. Harriet considered Charlotte her best friend and in 1852, they went together to Rome where Harriet studied sculpture. They created somewhat of a scandal by Harriet's male garb and their fondness for riding—astride. Both women managed to be succesful in their chosen careers: a remarkable fact considering the times, and further notable since they did not succumb to social pressure to adhere to the usual sex stereotypes.

1. quoted in Niven, Vern, "Artistic Paths that Crossed," THE LADDER, Vol. XI, No. 4, Jan. 1965, p. 15 [see cover for portraits]

HELEN POTTER
19th Century Mimic

She made a handsome living ($20,000/season) by impersonating favorites of the lyceum—she costumed, and did readings, humorous and heroic, imitating the manner and rhetoric of famous speakers with such accuracy she often fooled her audience into thinking they were seeing the real person! She imitated both men and women, made a fortune at the peak of her career and retired with no successor!

Pond, J.B., "Helen Potter," ECCENTRICITIES OF GENIUS, New York: Dillingham Co., 1900, p. 170

SARAH BERNHARDT
1844-1923/Actress

Born and educated in Paris, Bernhardt made her debut at age 17 at the Comédie Française. It was not, however, until 1867 and her portrayal of Cordelia in King Lear, that she began to attract the critics' attention. By 1877, "the divine Sarah" as Oscar Wilde dubbed her, had become "the Queen of the French stage in romance and classic tragedy." During the 1880's she began tours which spread her fame throughout Europe, England and the United States. In addition to acting, Bernhardt managed two theaters—the Théâtre de la Renaissance and the Théâtre Sarah Bernhardt (where she appeared as Hamlet) during the last decade of the 19th Century. The 20th Century brought motion pictures and Sarah played Queen Elizabeth and "la dame aux Camélias" in 1912. Undaunted by a leg amputation in 1915, she continued her career as an actress until shortly before her death in 1923. She wrote one play, L'Aveu in 1888 and her memoirs, which were translated and published in 1907. She has several biographers: Maurice Baring (1934) and Louis Verneuil (1942) among others.

[see p. 55 for portrait]

Explorers

HESTER STANHOPE
1776-1839/Explorer

She was six feet tall, as strong as an athlete and had a quick and incisive mind—a combination not found at all attractive in a late 18th Century woman. It was temporarily a dilemma to Stanhope, who wanted very much to have power and wealth in a time when the only women able to acquire either were "pretty" courtesans and simpering coquettes. Her answer was to become as dramatic and flamboyant as possible, to flaunt her unusual attributes and make them their own definition of beauty and value. She did as she pleased and fed the gossips a heady brew of free love rumours (all untrue until 1810!) "unwomanly" behavior such as dressing in men's clothes, and outspokenness to those she considered not worth her trouble. She managed to support her free life style until 1806, when her generous uncle William Pitt (Prime Minister of England) died. From 1806-1809, she tried to be a staid London "gentlewoman," but found it degrading and boring, and in 1810 set out for the East, from which she never returned. She, her lover Michael Bruce, and Elizabeth Williams, whom some also count as her lover, travelled through Turkey, Greece, Syria and Lebanon for several years, living on credit and a small annuity awarded her by parliament (at Pitt's dying request.) A legend grew up around her. She wore men's clothes, rode into Damascus unveiled, rode through the desert unmolested to ancient Queen Zenobia's Palmyra where she proclaimed herself Queen of the Arabs, visited harems, and was wined and dined by local sheiks and sultans. Finally, having achieved the recognition she felt her due, Stanhope decided to settle in the East and bought a convent (Djoun) in the Lebanese Mountains. Once ensconced, she refused to see Europeans, but opened the convent to all others, especially those interested in the occult, or poets. Her religion became a mixture of Moslem, Judaism and Christianity and she considered herself somewhat of a prophetess. The last eighteen years of her life were unhappy—her health deteriorated and her creditors dunned her. About a year before her death, she walled up all access to the outside of Djoun with the exception of a single door and forced almost all her servants to leave. When she died, alone, half-mad, hungry and penniless in 1839, she was buried on the side of a mountain, at night and with no ceremony.

Haslip, Joan, LADY H. STANHOPE, NY: Frederick A. Stokes, Co. 1936
Niven, Vern, "Queen of the Desert" THE LADDER, Vol. 10, No. 12, Sept. 1966, p. 18-21 [see p. 57 for portrait]

SACAJAWEA
1790-1884/ Guide & Explorer

Sacajawea was born along the shores of the Snake River, Idaho, a member of the Shoshone tribe. As a small child, she was captured by the Minnetarees of Knife River and taken to someplace near Bismark, North Dakota. There she was sold as a slave to Toussaint Chaboneau, an interpreter for the Northwest Fur Company. In 1804, when she was 14, she married Chaboneau. This same year, in October, Lewis and Clark reached Bismark on their way west and wanted to hire interpreters who knew the languages of the lands they wished to open up to colonization. They asked Sacajawea and Chaboneau to accompany them, more because they needed Sacajawea's Shoshone than Chaboneau's French, as is indicated by the fact that they delayed their departure almost eight months because of Sacajawea's pregnancy and eventual birth of a son, Feb. 11, 1805. During the journey, Sacajawea carried her son on her back, she canoed, hiked and climbed with him every step of the 5000 mile trip. At one point their canoe capsized and Chaboneau, paralyzed with fear and useless, began hysterically screaming. Sacajawea acted quickly and efficiently saved the pounds of valuable papers, instruments and medicines (which were irreplaceable without a backtrack of hundreds of miles) as Lewis and Clark record it in their journals. When she became ill, they camped until she recovered; she was essential to their exploration. When they reached her home ground she took over as their only guide. Her brother, Cameahwait, had become chief and she convinced him to supply the explorers' group with food, guides and information. When members of her tribe planned an attack on Lewis and Clark's camp, she was forwarned and guided them into totally unfamiliar wilderness where she kept them alive for several months by finding roots, berries, edible plants, and so forth. When they returned to North Dakota, Chaboneau was offered land and supplies in the east as payment, plus $500 in cash. Sacajawea received nothing but their thanks and some kind words in their journal of travels, "she who could divine routes,who had courage when the men failed . . ." [1] In 1877 Chaboneau was made an official interpreter at $300 a year, a comfortable and secure post. Six years before, Sacajawea had moved to Fremont County, Wyoming to live with her son on a reservation. She died there at 94 in 1884. All that commemorates her is a peak in Montana named after her by the Geological Survey and a statue in Oregon raised by the Daughters of the American Revolution.

1. *Humphrey, Grace, WOMEN IN AMERICAN HISTORY, Bobbs-Merrill Co., Indianapolis, 1919, p. 97* [see cover for portrait]

ANNIE S. PECK
1850-1935/Explorer & Scholar

A woman of many talents and diverse interest, Peck studied music in Germany from 1884-85, archaeology in Greece from 1885-86, was professor of Latin at Smith College and took up mountain climbing at the age of forty-five! In 1895, she ascended the Matterhorn and other Alpine peaks, and then turned her attention to peaks in South America; she climbed Mt. Sorata, Bolivia in 1904 (20,500 feet) and Huascarán in Peru in 1908 (21,812 feet). Huascaran was, at that time, the highest peak climbed by an American in the Western Hemisphere. The north peak of this mountain was named after her, and she was awarded a gold medal by the Peruvian government. Peck was a graduate of the University of Michigan, earning a B.A. in 1878 and an M.A. in 1881, and wrote several books about her South American travels.

Adelman, Joseph, "Annie Peck" FAMOUS WOMEN, New York: Ellis Lonow, Co., 1926, p. 292 [see p. 57 for portrait]

Artists

ROSA BONHEUR
1822-1899/Artist

Rosa was considered "incorrigible" and "indifferent to appearances and conventions" by her family, to whom these were distinctly negative characteristics. Her father tried to make her a dressmaker, and sent her off to a seminary to acquire "feminine virtues," but she was committed, even as a child, to painting: "I refused formally to learn to read, but before I was four years old I already had a passion for drawing, and I covered the white washed walls as high as I could reach with my shapeless sketches."[1] She knew what she wanted and at 13, her artist father agreed to teach her to paint. She made clay models and dissected dead animals to learn bone structure and musculature. Her passionate interest in animals led her to slaughter houses and stables, and she adopted masculine dress in order to come and go as she pleased in comfort, dressed in a way that suited her vision of herself. She never bothered to return to women's clothes, and in 1857, the Secretary General of France issued a permit which allowed her to dress as a man, legally. At the age of 19 (1841), she began exhibiting in Paris and for the next seven years exhibited both paintings and sculpture. They sold so well, she could afford to travel leisurely all over France, observing and sketching animals. In 1848, when her father died, she set up housekeeping with an aspiring artist, Nathalie Micas, and they were never again parted until Nathalie's death thirty years later. During this time she completed her transformation to masculine appearance by cutting her hair short. She had transformed herself so completely that during the last time she was wearing a skirt, she was arrested for female impersonation! At 31, her picture "Horse Fair" was sold for $8,000 and she was wealthy enough to buy a chateau where she and Nathalie tended an ever-enlarging menagerie of sheeps, goats, deer, gazelles, horses, cows, dogs, lions, boars, monkeys, parakeets, ponies from Iceland and mustangs from America—none in cages! During the Franco-Prussian war in 1870, she led a posse of "irregular guerillas" made up of "poachers, wood-cutters, charcoal burners . . . " and opened her house to all French. She'd been given three awards during her lifetime: 1845, the Beaux Arts medal, 1865, the ribbon of the Legion of Honor, and thirty years later, the cross.

Damon, Gene & Stuart, Lee, "Lesbian Artist: Rosa Bonheur" THE
LADDER, Vol. 6, No. 2, Nov. 1961, pp. 9-10
Foss, Kenelm, "Rosa Bonheur" UNWEDDED BLISS, Kingswood, Surrey:
The World's Work, 1949, p. 34   [see cover for portrait]

MARY CASSATT
1845-1926/Artist

Cassatt had one passion in her life: art. In all things she was
obedient, conventional and quiet except this. "I was born with a
passion for line and color," she told her father when explaining
why she was so determined to go to art school rather than become
a "perfect lady," as he wished. And in her art she defied
convention as radically as she could. She became an ardent
supporter and admirer of the Impressionists, especially Degas, and
began to experiment in her own paintings with their new style,
eventually developing one of her own (which gave her the label,
"Independent"). She ceased submitting to the traditional and
prestigious "Salon" (where she had been very successful) and made
her way in the unknown and often hostile atmosphere of the
avant-gardists. She was taken note of, but not as much as the men
were, and the French considered her a foreigner and the
Americans, an expatriate. She didn't fit but she continued painting
and eventually won some recognition, albeit praise with faint
damns: "Mary Cassatt offers us a circumscribed Jamesian world of
well-bred ladies living lives of leisure, delighting in their dresses,
their company and their well-behaved children. There is an odd
contrast between the boldness of her style and the world of
perpetual afternoon tea it serves to record," wrote Edgar P.
Richardson in "Art News" (Vol. 53, pp. 21-23, April, '54). She
won two prizes, the Lippincott and Norman Wait Harriss Prizes,
but refused them both on grounds that it was not ethical to single
out an individual artist for a special prize. She did accept being
made Chevalier of the Legion of Honor because it was difficult to
get the honor awarded to a woman. As she grew old, Cassatt found
herself in an "alien art world." She did not understand or
appreciate the Cubists it would seem, and when Degas died in
1917, she mourned "the last great artist of the 19th Century."

Carson, Julia, MARY CASSATT, New York: David McKay Co., 1966

See Also: Harriet Hosmer

Additional Bibliography

In addition to books mentioned in the text . . .

On Specific Women:

Abigail Adams:
Holloway, Laura, THE LADIES OF THE WHITE HOUSE. Boston: 1881
Whitney, Janet, ABIGAIL ADAMS, Boston: 1947

L.M. Alcott:
Alcott, L.M., HER LIFE, LETTERS AND JOURNALS, Cheney, Ednah, ed., Boston: 1923
Alcott, L.M., AUNT JO'S SCRAP BAG. Boston: 1900

Angelica Balabanoff:
Balabonoff, A., MY LIFE AS A REBEL

Mary M. Bethune:
Carruth, Ella, SHE WANTED TO READ
Holt, Rackham, MARY M. BETHUNE

E.G. Flynn:
Flynn, E.G. I SPEAK MY OWN PIECE

Margaret Fuller:
Fuller, M., MEMOIRS OF M. FULLER OSSOLI. N.Y.: 1869
Fuller, M., WRITINGS OF MARGARET FULLER. Wade, Mason, ed., N.Y.: 1941
Wade, Mason, MARGARET FULLER, WHETSTONE OF GENIUS, N.Y.: 1940

Shikibu Murasaki:
DIARIES OF COURT LADIES, Shepley, Annie, (translator) N.Y.: 1920

Constance Markievicz:
Markievicz, C., PRISON LETTERS, London: 1934 and Toronto

Sarojini Naidu:
Naidu, S. THE SCEPTERED FLUTE, N.Y.: 1928

Sylvia Pankhurst:
Pankhurst, S., THE SUFFRAGE MOVEMENT: AN INTIMATE ACCOUNT OF PERSONS AND IDEAS, N.Y.: 1931

Emmeline Pankhurst:
Pankhurst, E., MY OWN STORY, London: 1914

Margaret Sanger:
Sanger, Margaret, MY FIGHT FOR BIRTH CONTROL, N.Y.: 1931

Sanger, Margaret, HAPPINESS IN MARRIAGE, N.Y.: 1926 and many others . . .
Lader, L., MARGARET SANGER: PIONEER OF BIRTH CONTROL

Frances Wright:
Wright (D'Arusmont) Frances, VIEWS OF SOCIETY AND MANNERS IN AMERICA, (letters), London: 1821

Books of General Interest:
Catt, Carrie, WOMAN SUFFRAGE AND POLITICS, Seattle: 1969
Chesnut, M.B., A DIARY FROM DIXIE, Boston: 1949
Dell, Floyd, WOMEN AS WORLD BUILDERS, Chicago: 1913
Flexner, E., CENTURY OF STRUGGLE, N.Y.: 1968
Irwin, Inez, ANGELS & AMAZONS, N.Y.: 1933
Meyer, G., THE SCIENTIFIC LADY IN ENGLAND, Berkeley: 1955
Mill, Joahn and Harriet, essays on sex equality, Chicago: 1970
O'Neill, William, THE WOMAN MOVEMENT
Putnam, E., THE LADY, Chicago: 1970
Schreiner, O., WOMAN AND LABOR, N.Y. 1911
Schreiner, O., WOMAN AND WAR, N.Y.: 1911
Scott, Anne (ed.), THE AMERICAN WOMAN: WHO WAS SHE? New Jersey: 1971
Diner, Helen, MOTHERS AND AMAZONS
Newly reprinted by Source Book Press, New York:
THE HISTORY OF WOMAN SUFFRAGE (12 vols.)—edited by E.C. Stanton, S.B. Anthony, M.J. Gage and I.H. Harper

And, from Times Change Press:
Goldman, Emma, THE TRAFFIC IN WOMEN (AND OTHER ESSAYS ON FEMINISM) ($1.35)
Negrin, Su, A GRAPHIC NOTEBOOK ON FEMINISM ($1.25)
Kisner, Arlene, WOODHULL & CLAFLIN'S WEEKLY ($1.35)

● ● ●

Author's Note

99% of this pamphlet was put together from secondary sources (most written by men—many of whom were defiantly sexist and all of whom were biased). Some facts and/or personalities may have been left out—because of (1) difficulty in finding reliable sources (2) space (3) my own feminist biases. I've tried to be honest and fair; my apologies for any relevant/crucial omissions.

Index